THE CORE CURRICULUM

Gordon Kirk

LONDONTON TORONTO

Changing Perspectives in Education

Series Editor: Noel Entwistle, BSc, PhD

The Core Curriculum   Gordon Kirk
Teaching Study Skills   Ian Selmes
Understanding Classroom Learning   Noel Entwistle
Research on Education   John Nisbet
Appraising Teacher Quality   John Wilson

British Library Cataloguing in Publication Data

Kirk, Gordon
    The core curriculum.—(Changing
    perspectives in education)
    1. Education—Great Britain—
    Curricula
    I. Title   II. Series
    375'.00941   LB1564.G7

    ISBN 0 340 39516 8

First published 1986

Copyright © 1986 Gordon Kirk

Photoset by
Rowland Phototypesetting Ltd,
Bury St Edmunds, Suffolk.
Printed in Great Britain
for Hodder and Stoughton Educational,
a division of Hodder and Stoughton Ltd,
Mill Road, Dunton Green, Sevenoaks, Kent by
Richard Clay (The Chaucer Press), Bungay Suffolk

Contents

The Series Editor

Noel Entwistle is Bell Professor of Education at Edinburgh University and Director of the Godfrey Thomson Unit for Educational Research. Previously he was Professor of Educational Research at Lancaster University and editor of the *British Journal of Educational Psychology*. His main research interests are in the field of study learning and motivation, and he currently chairs the Innovation, Research and Development Committee of the Scottish Microelectronics in Education Committee.

Changing Perspectives in Education

This series examines changing perspectives on a variety of educational issues and practices. It seeks to make accessible to the teacher and administrator, as well as to students, the most recent thinking, research, and development work in those areas. In education, ideas are presented all too often in a one-sided fashion, using rhetoric to disguise the lack of serious thought or supportive evidence. This series seeks to provoke balanced discussion on current issues based on a careful analysis of the most recent relevant information and research evidence.

The intention is to place current issues critically in an historical context but only so as to emphasise the changes which have subsequently taken place and the choices which currently face us. Recent thinking is described in as non-technical a way as the topic allows, with the emphasis on presenting complex ideas thoroughly but palatably. Practical examples are used to illustrate the theoretical ideas being presented, and so make the classroom and curricular applications more immediately apparent. Recognising the limited time teachers and administrators have, the series tries to cover each topic in a concise manner, indicating additional reading and references to more detailed information wherever appropriate.

The Author

Gordon Kirk is the Principal of Moray House College of Education in Edinburgh. Previously he was a lecturer in Education at Aberdeen University before becoming Head of the Education Department at Jordanhill College, Glasgow. He was a member of the Munn Committee which considered how to improve the balance of the secondary school curriculum in Scotland. He is a member of the Consultative Committee on the Curriculum which advises the Secretary of State for Scotland on curriculum matters, and of the General Teaching Council for Scotland. He is also currently Chairman of the Scottish Council for Research in Education and of the School Broadcasting Council for Scotland.

Preface

What should children and young people learn at school? Does society have the right to expect that all school leavers should have reached certain levels of competence? Who should determine what these levels of competence should be? How might schools be made more responsive to changing social and technological demands? To what extent can teachers be made more accountable to the communities they serve?

For some, the answer to all of these questions is clear: there should be introduced a national core curriculum which all schools should be expected to teach. For others, that solution is totally unacceptable: it undermines the professional autonomy of teachers; it threatens the transformation of schools into agencies for political indoctrination; and it obliterates the diversity and variety which are characteristic of our traditional educational arrangements.

This book seeks to unravel the major issues involved and invites the reader to form an independent judgement. Its intended readership encompasses student-teachers in schools, teachers in schools, those who are responsible at different levels of the educational service for curriculum policy and for establishing relationships between policy and classroom practice, as well as the general reader. To all of these groups the book offers an analysis of principles and of their relationship to professional action.

From a consideration of the growth of central government influence on the school curriculum in Chapter 1, the book moves, in Chapter 2, to an examination of the case for a national curriculum framework. That case is then examined in Chapter 3 by adducing six counter arguments and testing the validity of each of these in turn. On the basis of that analysis, Chapter 4 derives a set of criteria that may be used to evaluate proposals for a national curriculum framework. These criteria are illustrated in action in the consideration of three current proposals for a national core curriculum – those emanating from Australia, from Scotland, and from England and Wales. Finally, in Chapter 6, the major themes of the book are drawn together to outline a new synthesis in which traditional dichotomies and polarisations of view are reconciled.

The aim throughout the book is not to provide a one-sided defence of a national curriculum framework, but rather to develop, through the analysis of the issues, a means whereby proposals for a national curriculum framework may be evaluated.

Acknowledgments

A book of this kind is at once a contribution to, and a product of, a tradition of critical reflection on the school curriculum: it represents a distillation, by a single author, of a host of ideas and insights that have grown out of countless interactions with students, teachers, colleagues and others. I happily acknowledge my indebtedness to the very many individuals, known and unknown, who have influenced the analysis which the book seeks to provide. At the same time, there are individuals whose assistance and support were of a direct and specific kind and I wish to record my gratitude to them. Professor Noel Entwistle made many helpful suggestions on the structure and tone of the book and subjected the penultimate version to detailed scrutiny and comment. Hazel Robertson and David Fairgrieve, both on the staff of Moray House College library, willingly hunted down all kinds of references for me and could not have been more obliging. Mary Swinton, with patience and efficiency, typed and retyped the manuscript. Finally, I owe a special debt of gratitude to my wife and family, who allowed the writing of the book to intrude rather drastically into time that should have been devoted to more important matters.

1

The Growth of Central Influence
on the Curriculum

The Historical Context

Who should determine what young people learn at school? That has
been a keenly disputed question in Britain for more than a hundred
years. As public education developed in the middle of tthe
nineteenth century, and as public funds were allocated for this
purpose, it was considered that central government should oversee
what was taught in schools. If investment in public education was a
necessary political and humanitarian response to the problems of
poverty and underprivilege, if it was an appropriate means of
fostering and maintaining religious adherence, and if it was calcu-
lated to equip young people with the skills demanded by a changing
industrial society, then a strategy had to be found for ensuring that
value was obtained for the funds invested. According to the New-
castle Commission of 1861, the best means of obtaining that assurance was

> to institute a searching examination by a competent authority of
> every child in every school to which grants are to be paid with the
> view of ascertaining whether these indispensable elements of
> knowledge are thoroughly acquired and to make the prospects
> and position of the teacher dependent, to a considerable extent,
> on the results of this examination.[1]

In 1862 the Revised Code instituted a system of grants for schools:
8s. (40p) per year was to be awarded for every pupil who attended
more than 200 times. Moreover, all pupils were to be subject to

annual tests in reading, writing and arithmetic, administered by HMI, and 2s. 8d. (approximately 14p) was to be deducted from the grant for each test a child failed. Such were the main features of the strategy known as 'payment by results'. Through that strategy the machinery of the state was deployed to control the work of teachers, to prescribe standards of achievement in a narrow range of objectives, and representatives of the central government were required to judge whether or not these standards had been achieved.

The system of payment by results was abolished in 1895. Nevertheless, central control of the elementary school curriculum was maintained through a succession of codes and it was not until 1936 that these regulations were changed in a way which left responsibility for 'a suitable curriculum and syllabus with due regard to the organisation and circumstances of the school' in the hands of teachers. Indeed, as far as secondary schools were concerned, the stranglehold exerted by central government over the curriculum was not relaxed until the 1944 Education Act for England and Wales and the corresponding Scottish legislation of 1945.

While the system of 'payment by results' was formally abolished in 1895 it has continued over the years to represent an enormous affront to the professional consciousness of teachers and a threat to the creation of an effective educational service. There are three grounds for this pervasive professional opposition to the system. First, 'payment by results' demeaned education and reduced it to a mere cramming exercise in which all that is expected of pupils is a capacity for recall. Secondly, the system circumscribed professional activity, constrained initiative, and demanded acquiescence in a curriculum that was so narrowly conceived as to represent a parody of education. Finally, 'payment by results' has been interpreted to exemplify a state-controlled curriculum, the deliberate use of political power to mould the minds of the young. For these reasons, 'payment by results' has remained anathema to teachers and their professional associations. Consequently, any measure which seeks to strengthen central influence on the curriculum and to weaken teachers' autonomy in curriculum matters is still likely to evince the same suspicion and hostility with which teachers responded to 'payment by results'. This deeply ingrained suspicion of central government explains the aversion of teachers to any increase of ministerial involvement in curricular matters.

In the years between 1862 and 1944/45 there was a significant lessening of central control of the school curriculum; the years since then have witnessed an equally significant shift in the opposite direction. The extent of that shift can be illustrated by two ministerial pronouncements. The first, attributed to George Tomlinson, the Minister of Education from 1947 in the post-war Labour government, intimated with concise frankness that the 'Minister knows nowt about curriculum'. The second, uttered by Sir Keith Joseph, the Conservative Secretary of State for Education and Science in the present government, in a speech at Sheffield in January 1984 was no less frank:

> I can offer an account of what the minimum level to be attained at 16 by 80%–90% of pupils would entail in a few areas of the curriculum . . . ; in English, pupils would need to demonstrate that they are attentive listeners and confident speakers when dealing with everyday matters of which they have experience, that they can read straightforward written information and pass it on – orally and in written form – without loss of meaning and that they can say clearly what their own views are; in Mathematics, that they can apply the topics and skills in the foundation list proposed in the Cockcroft Report; in Science, that they are willing and able to take a practical approach to problems, involving sensible observations and appropriate measurements and can communicate their findings effectively . . .; in History, that they possess some historical knowledge and perspective, understand the concepts of cause and consequence, and can compare and extract information from historical evidence and be aware of its limitations; and in CDT (Craft, Design and Technology), that they can design and make something, using a limited range of materials and calling on a restricted range of concepts and give an account of what they have done and the problems they encountered.[2]

The first statement, evoking a tradition of political non-interference in the curriculum, repudiates the locus of central government in such matters. The second, by contrast, is a striking use of ministerial authority to influence what is taught in the schools and is indicative of the assertive pursuit of government policy to wield such influence. This chapter seeks to chart the growth of that government assertiveness and to highlight some of the significant manifestations of its emergence.

James Callaghan's Ruskin Speech 1976

There is evidence that, traditionally, ministers in successive governments were persuaded to adopt a neutral stance on the curriculum. One indeed, the Conservative Minister David Eccles, is reputed to have alluded to 'the secret garden of the curriculum'. That metaphor of the curriculum as forbidden territory to ministers was directly challenged by Mr Callaghan's speech at Ruskin College, Oxford, in October 1976. The Prime Minister was clearly motivated by growing public concern about education and the work of the schools. His brief for the speech was prepared by the DES and was leaked to the press in advance. The Yellow Paper, as the leaked document came to be called, was critical of teaching in primary and secondary schools. It claimed that some teachers in the primary school had allowed performance in the basic skills of reading, writing and arithmetic to be adversely affected by their inadequate understanding and hence uncritical application of child-centred, or informal, methods. With regard to the secondary school curriculum, the Yellow Paper maintained that too much scope had been given to the principle of pupil choice, with the result that many pupils were following unbalanced programmes and not enough pupils were studying science-based and technological subjects. The antidote to these ills was thought to lie in the institution of a core or common component in the curriculum of all pupils.

The Prime Minister's speech was eagerly anticipated by the educational and wider community and it duly received the full media treatment. However, if people expected a lucid analysis of the ills of contemporary education, together with appropriate and carefully contrived proposals for change, they were disappointed. The speech had more modest objectives. First, it implicitly and explicitly asserted that the aims of education and the content of the curriculum were legitimate matters for public discussion and could not to be looked upon as the exclusive concern of professionals:

> I take it that no-one claims exclusive rights in this field. Public interest is strong and legitimate and will be satisfied . . . Parents, teachers, learned and professional bodies, representatives of

higher education and both sides of industry, together with the government, all have an important part to play in formulating and expressing the purpose of education and the standards that we need.[3]

Of course, the very fact that the Prime Minister made the speech at all, and that he had rejected the advice 'to keep off the grass', as he put it, was a powerful reinforcement of the case he was arguing. Secondly, the speech identified issues that, in the Prime Minister's judgement, were the source of public concern and required public debate. Among the issues raised were the following: deficiency in the basic skills amongst school leavers; the reluctance of many of our best trained students to join industry; standards of literacy and numeracy; the value of informal teaching methods; the place of 'a basic curriculum with universal standards'; and 'the role of the Inspectorate in relation to national standards'. Very clearly, the Prime Minister saw the speech as an opportunity to set the agenda for an extended public discussion of educational issues. The 'Great Debate' followed.

The Great Debate 1976–77

The Great Debate took place at two levels. First, it was represented by a massive output of articles in the educational and the national press about standards, about the composition of the core curriculum, about the control of the curriculum, and about the role of the schools and other related matters. Secondly, at a more formal level, it took the form of eight regional one-day conferences. To each of these there were invited about 200 representatives of the world of industry and commerce, trade unions, teachers' associations, local education authorities and institutions of higher education. The background paper for these meetings, *Educating our Children: Four Subjects for Debate*, was prepared by the DES. This derived clearly from the issues raised in the Prime Minister's Ruskin speech. The four subjects for debate were:

the school curriculum 5–16
the assessment of standards
the education and training of teachers
school and working life.

Among the issues for discussion of the first two subjects were the following:

What should be the aims and content of a core curriculum?
How best can an agreed core curriculum be put into effect?
Do we have adequate means of obtaining reliable information about the performance of pupils in schools and, if not, what further measures are required?

What value was served by these regional conferences? According to one commentator, the format allowed little more than 'a short canter for a stable of hobby horses'.[4] Another verdict was that the Great Debate was 'a unique exercise in contemplating the country's educational navel'.[5] For her part, the Minister, Shirley Williams, expressed satisfaction at this move towards open consultation on the part of the DES. It is not beyond the bounds of possibility that the regional conferences demonstrated such a diversity of views on important aspects of educational policy that the way was left clear for a more decisive lead from the centre. That lead was speedily forthcoming.

Education in Schools: A Consultative Document (The Green Paper) July 1977

The Green Paper from the Department of Education and Science and the Welsh Office demonstrates its relationship to the Ruskin speech and to the issues raised in the Great Debate before moving swiftly to a statement on the partnership between schools, local education authorities and ministers. That statement includes the following justification for central involvement in curriculum matters:

The Secretaries of State are responsible in law for the promotion of the education of the people of England and Wales. They need to know what is being done by the local education authorities and, through them, what is happening in the schools. They must draw attention to national needs if they believe the educational system is not adequately meeting them.

Then, after alluding to current criticisms of the curriculum, and having asserted the need 'to establish generally accepted principles for the composition of the school curriculum for all pupils', the paper continues:

> It would not be compatible with the duty of the Secretaries of State to 'promote the education of the people of England and Wales', or with their accountability to Parliament, to abdicate from leadership on educational issues which have become a matter of lively public concern. The Secretaries of State will therefore seek to establish a broad agreement with their partners in the educational service on a framework for the curriculum, and in particular on whether, because there are aims common to all schools and to all pupils at certain stages, there should be a 'core' or 'protected' part.

In execution of that policy it was proposed that a circular would be issued to all local authorities asking them to carry out a review of the curriculum in their areas in consultation with their schools and to report the results within about twelve months.

Enquiry into Local Education Authority Arrangements for the Management of the Curriculum

Circular 14.27 was a wide-ranging questionnaire to LEAs covering all aspects of the planning, development, evaluation and resourcing of the curriculum in their schools. Some of the relevant questions were as follows:

> What procedures have the authority established to enable them to carry out their curricular responsibilities under Section 23 of the Education Act (1944)?

> What systematic arrangements, if any, have the authority established for the collection of information about the curricula offered by schools in their area?

> How does the authority help schools decide on the relative emphasis they should give to particular aspects of the curriculum, especially the promotion of literacy and numeracy?

> What contribution has the authority made to the consideration of the problems faced by secondary schools, of providing suitable subject options for older pupils while avoiding the premature

dropping of curricular elements regarded as essential for all pupils?

What curricular elements does the authority regard as essential?

The replies to the circular were reported in 1979. Two significant findings emerged in relation to the questions quoted above. First, 'most authorities do not have systematic arrangements for regularly collecting and monitoring curricular information from their schools'. Secondly, there was very considerable diversity of view as to what the 'essential elements' of the curriculum should be, many authorities regarding such matters as being the concern of the schools themselves. Given the prevailing views about where responsibility for curricula rested, these findings are not perhaps totally unpredictable. Indeed, one critic of the exercise considered that 'the circular was a device which managed to make LEAs look as if they were failing in their duties, and thus allowed the DES to take the initiative'.[6] For their part, the ministers concerned made their intentions clear. They proposed 'to give a lead in the process of reaching a national consensus on a desirable framework for the curriculum'. Such an initiative would 'give central government a firmer basis for the development of national policies and the deployment of resources; and provide a checklist for authorities and schools in formulating and reviewing their curricular aims and policies in the light of local needs and circumstances . . . Conceived in this way, an agreed framework could offer a significant step forward in the quest for improvement in the consistency and quality of school education across the country.'[7] As a first step in the development of such a framework, HMI would be invited to formulate 'a view of a possible curriculum on the basis of their knowledge of schools'.

Papers from HM Inspectorate

The writings of HM Inspectorate can be seen to reinforce the commitment to a national framework for the curriculum. In 1977 they produced *Curriculum 11–16*. The first section of that document set out a powerful 'case for a common curriculum in secondary education to 16'. Such a common curriculum was thought to derive from eight 'areas of experience':

the aesthetic and creative
the ethical
the linguistic
the mathematical
the physical
the scientific
the social and political
the spiritual.

The Inspectorate maintained their attack on the 'unacceptable variety' of curricular provision in their *Aspects of Secondary Education* (1979) and again in *A View of The Curriculum* (1980). The latter document re-emphasised the need for a national curriculum framework and for the delineation of a common core of learning for all pupils. The composition of that core was put forward, rather tentatively, as a series of 'propositions for consideration'. In effect, the inspectorate proposed a core that consisted of English, Mathematics, Religious Education, Physical Education, Modern Languages, 'Arts and Applied Crafts', History, and Science subjects. Finally, in *The Curriculum from 5 to 16* (1985) the Inspectorate insisted that throughout the period of compulsory schooling all pupils should maintain contact with nine areas of learning – the 1977 list, except that 'technological' learning is added and 'the social and political' is replaced by 'the human and social'. In each of these areas of learning schools were urged to cultivate appropriate knowledge, concepts, skills and attitudes, thus ensuring that all pupils received a broadly comparable educational experience.

The National Curriculum Framework

The government made its first attempt at formulating a national curriculum framework in the consultative document *A Framework for the School Curriculum* (1980). In a somewhat terse paper – it being considered that the more substantial analysis of principles had been carried out in the HMI document *A View of the Curriculum* – it was maintained that throughout the period of compulsory schooling, from 5–16, all pupils should undertake study in English, Mathematics, Science, Religious Education, and Physical Education. At the secondary level, the report continued, pupils should study in addition a modern language and the curriculum of all pupils should include what is called 'preparation for adult and working life', a varied programme of activities incorporating Craft, Design and Technology, History and Geography, Moral Education, Health Education, and 'preparation for parenthood and for a participatory role in adult society'.

The government's thinking was further developed in *The School Curriculum* (1981), which was clearly seen as the culminating point of several years of public discussion. Having reasserted the need for a national framework and having listed a set of general educational aims, the ministers set out 'the approach to the curriculum which they consider should now be followed in the years ahead'. As far as the primary phase of schooling was concerned, the plan of development favoured the same activities as were listed in *A Framework for the School Curriculum*, except that more attention was devoted to History and Geography, to Expressive Arts, and to Science, and to the need for clearly structured and progressively demanding work in these areas of the curriculum. The framework for the secondary school curriculum was taken to comprise English, Mathematics, Science, Modern Languages, Microelectronics, Craft, Design and Technology, Religious Education, Physical Education, Humanities, Practical and Aesthetic activities, and 'preparation for adult life'.

The paper was seen as constituting 'guidance for local education authorities' and the ministers proposed to inform themselves in due course about the action taken by LEAs with regard to that guidance. That was reinforced in a subsequent circular to LEAs later in 1981 and two years later Circular 8/83 sought a progress report from LEAs on the formation of a curriculum policy for pupils of all abilities and aptitudes.

While *The School Curriculum* might have been seen as the government's definitive statement on the structure of the national curriculum framework, it was superseded in September 1984 by *The Organisation and Content of the 5–16 Curriculum*, although the wording of the latest document conveyed the impression that the final nature and scope of the national framework has not yet been determined. The structure of the curriculum proposed for the primary phase is similar to that set out in earlier documentation but includes the following additional components:

Craft and practical work leading to some experience of design and technology and of solving problems;
introduction to computers;
insights into the adult world, including how people earn their living.

The proposed structure for the secondary phase is similar to that in *The School Curriculum* except that specific provision is made in the latest document for Home Economics for all pupils.

There is one feature of these developments that is worth highlighting. Throughout the official documents there is a disclaimer about the government's intention. Repeatedly it is urged that there is no intention to introduce, through legislation, a nationally prescribed curriculum that would be binding on all LEAs and on all schools. Thus, *Curriculum 11–16* (1977) from HMI avers:

> We repeat that it is not the intention to advocate a standard curriculum for all secondary schools to the age of 16, not least because that would be educationally naive. One of the greatest assets of our educational arrangements is the freedom of schools to respond to differing circumstances in their localities and to encourage the enterprise and strength of their teachers.

Indeed, the government's own document, *The School Curriculum* (1981), includes these words: 'Neither the government nor the local authorities should specify in detail what the schools should teach.' At the same time, there is evidence that the government's interest in the school curriculum was not limited to the institution of a national framework. The White Paper, *Better Schools* (1985), indicated that one of the government's major policy commitments was 'to secure greater clarity about the objectives and content of the curriculum', that being considered a necessary step towards the improvement of standards achieved by pupils. That policy is being pursued in two ways: first, the DES is publishing a series of documents on the objectives to be sought in the different areas of the curriculum. To date, the documentation has appeared on English (DES, 1984)[8] and Science (DES, 1985).[9] Both documents seek to identify the skills and understandings which their respective subjects should seek to achieve at different stages of schooling. Secondly, ministers have approved 'national criteria' for different subject areas. These national criteria have been designed in connection with the new General Certificate of Secondary Education and are intended to 'offer a concise account of the understanding, knowledge and competences which should be developed in the course of following the syllabus'. Without question, these developments will impose very powerful constraints on the schools and mark a decisive shift of power in curricular matters to the centre. It is not surprising that a leading official of the NUT should dismiss the White Paper which collates the present government's curricular initiatives as 'a dose of centralist rhetoric'.[10]

For its part, the government insists that 'the establishment of broadly agreed objectives would not mean that the curricular policies of the Secretary of State, the LEA and the school should relate to each other in a nationally uniform way. In the government's view, such diversity is healthy, accords well with the English and Welsh traditions of school education and makes for liveliness and innovation.'[11]

Arguably, what has occurred is a reinterpretation of the traditional partnership between central government, LEAs and schools which has allowed central government, on the basis of its 'accountability to parliament for the performance of the educational service at all levels', progressively to nudge LEAs into a fuller appreciation of their curricular responsibilities and, through that, to influence the schools. The strategy consisted not of ministerial diktat but the progressive application of pressure on LEAs to ensure that the school curriculum in their areas was in line with a real or imagined consensus about what pupils should learn at school. At the same time, there were other events which very considerably strengthened the lead from the centre and made it more likely that LEAs would respond positively to the government's initiatives. These are considered in the remainder of this chapter.

The Demise of the Schools Council

The Schools Council (for curriculum and examinations), was established in 1964 by the Secretary of State for Education and Science as an independent body with the function of 'the promotion of education by carrying out research into, and keeping under review, curricula, teaching methods and examinations in schools'. It was funded jointly by the DES and LEAs and its membership was deliberately designed to achieve a majority of teachers. Over the years, the Schools Council was responsible for a prodigious output of reports and materials on every aspect of the school curriculum. It very definitely constituted the most significant and influential curriculum development agency in the country and many of its projects attracted international acclaim.

In keeping with its standing as an independent body with a built-in majority of teachers, the Council was committed to the thesis that 'each school should have the fullest measure of responsibility for its own curriculum and teaching methods based on the needs of its own pupils and evolved by its own staff'. It saw its function not to produce curricular prescriptions but rather 'to extend the range of possibilities open to teachers, and to provide them with the most detailed research evidence on which their judgement can be exercised'.[12] Indeed, even when the Schools Council diverted its attention to the whole curriculum, in contrast to its preoccupation with individual areas or aspects, it maintained its non-recommendatory stance. *The Whole Curriculum* (1975) and *The Practical Curriculum* (1981) both sought to alert teachers to the complex issues that have to be taken into account in whole curriculum planning, but both eschewed the provision of ready-made answers. The Schools Council could therefore be seen as testifying vigorously to two principles – curriculum diversity and teacher control of the curriculum.

Over the years, the relationship between the DES and the Schools Council was characterised by what one commentator has described as 'captiousness'. The confidential Yellow Paper, indeed, dismissed the achievements of the Council as 'generally mediocre'. Reservations continued to be expressed about the power of teacher unions in the Council and there were those who felt that 'the curriculum was too important to be left to teachers'. In October 1981, the government's review of the Schools Council, conducted by Mrs Nancy Trenaman, concluded that, although the Council had been 'too political, too complicated and was over-stretched', it should nevertheless continue in existence, albeit in a slimmer form. Notwithstanding that report, conducted on behalf of the government, Sir Keith Joseph intimated in April 1982 that he proposed to terminate the Schools Council and to institute two new bodies – the

School Curriculum Development Committee and the Secondary Examinations Council – to carry out certain advisory functions relating to the curriculum on the one hand and examinations on the other. Sir Keith made it clear that the membership of the two new committees would comprise 'persons nominated by the Secretary of State for their fitness for this particular important responsibility'. That was the ministerial response to Mrs Trenaman's claim that 'a nominated body is consistent . . . with a system of central government control of curriculum and examinations'. In the Commons debate which followed the ministerial announcement, there were some MPs who welcomed the demise of 'a nonsensical curriculum development body that has done nothing but damage education over the years'. Others, however, objected to the replacement of the Schools Council by two unelected bodies; they saw dangers in the minister 'surrounding himself by people of one opinion', and in the 'centralised patronage' which was said to characterise the new arrangements, and they detected the eclipse of the values of curriculum pluralism for which the Schools Council had stood.[13] Indeed, one commentator has maintained that the very success of the Schools Council may have hastened its downfall. 'It is ironic that the Council's projects, most of them in one way or another emphasising the value of local initiative, teacher involvement, school-level decision-making and various innovations in pedagogy such as interdisciplinary teaching, should lead to heightened activity nationally to control the curriculum.'[14]

The Rise of the Assessment of Performance Unit (APU)

The APU was instituted by the DES in 1974 'to promote the development of methods of assessing and monitoring the achievements of children at school, and to seek to identify the incidence of under-achievement'. While the birth of the new unit was intimated in a document dealing with educational disadvantage and the educational needs of immigrants, the work of the unit has very clearly been concerned with the more general question of standards of achievement in schools. The proponents of the APU insisted that government is bound to maintain an interest in the quality of education in order to determine whether resources are being rationally deployed and whether the schools are serving the changing needs of pupils and of society. To that end, ways had to be found of monitoring the achievements of pupils.

The initial strategy planned by APU was to examine pupils' performances not in the recognised school subjects but in certain areas of development – the verbal, mathematical, scientific, ethical (subsequently changed to social and personal), aesthetic and physical. To date, surveys of achievement have been undertaken in language (with separate provision for foreign languages), mathematics, and science, but not in the three remaining areas. Jean Dawson, administrative head of APU, summarises the achievements of the unit in these words:

> We have now carried out successfully a total of 27 national surveys without undue disruption to schools, with the general support of the LEAs and teachers concerned . . . and with the enthusiastic cooperation of the children we have tested . . ..
> Many of the suspicions which existed when the unit was set up, both about the political motivation for its creation and the likely effects of national monitoring on the curriculum, have been allayed (if not entirely put to rest) by the way in which the exercise has been carried out, by the sensitivities displayed by the monitoring teams, by the way in which groups of teachers up and down the country have been involved in the development, trialling and pre-testing of materials, and by the cool, impartial way in which the results have been presented.[15]

At the same time there were others who were resolutely opposed to the APU and its philosophy. They doubted whether valid measures of *all* of the areas of development could be devised; they maintained that the tests used would have a distorting and trivialising effect on pupils' learning ('this year's test becomes next year's curriculum'); they pointed to the possibility, notwithstanding the assurances that light sampling techniques would be deployed, that superficial comparisons would be made on the basis of inadequate evidence between areas and between schools; and they detected in the paraphernalia of mass testing associated with the APU the most sinister intrusion of central government into the work of the schools and the spectre of state-controlled curricula.

The Reform of the Examination System at 16+

It is widely acknowledged that the school examination system has exerted a powerful controlling effect on school curricula, even if, in more recent times, CSE (Mode 3) has allowed schools to play a significant role on the assessment of their own pupils. While, for many years, there has been discussion, in the Schools Council and elsewhere, about the reform of the examination system and the closer integration of CSE and GCE, Sir Keith Joseph gave notice in January 1984 of much more radical changes in the assessment of pupils at the end of compulsory schooling. He envisaged a shift, in line with modern educational thinking, away from a system in which pupils are assessed in relation to each other (a norm-referenced system) to one in which they would be assessed in relation to certain pre-specified criteria (a criterion-referenced system). In the latter, pupils succeed or 'pass' if they reach certain levels of competence: they are expected to give evidence of having reached a particular level of performance regardless of how they stand in relation to their peers. These features will characterise the new General Certificate of Secondary Education in England and Wales.

Sir Keith Joseph has intimated that 'national' criteria will be established in the main curriculum areas. This development will clearly call for detailed research in order to establish clearly and unambiguously the skills and understandings testified by a given level of achievement. In this way, a system is expected to evolve in which teachers, employers, further and higher education, as well as pupils, can have confidence in what a given award actually means: it will indicate, clearly, what a pupil has been able to achieve. Whether or not a reform of this kind will lead, as Sir Keith Joseph maintained, to a general raising of standards of achievement, it has been interpreted as a further encroachment on the part of central government into what is taught and learned in schools. Indeed, if performance criteria are to be *national*, if they are to have currency throughout the system, and if they are to be as detailed and specific as the proponents of criterion-referenced testing insist, then this reform presages central intervention in the school curriculum of a most emphatic kind.

Government Policy on Standards

As has been noted, signs of a more active interest of central government in the school curriculum were apparent under the Labour administration in the 1970s. It is arguable that this interest has intensified under the present Conservative government. That government made standards in education a principal plank in its election platform and the action undertaken by that government in relation to curriculum and assessment is part of a wider and coherent strategy on standards in education. That strategy incorporates a review of the content of courses of initial teacher training; the establishment of a committee for the accreditation of courses of teacher education; an inquiry into the procedures for the external validation of courses in public sector higher education; an inquiry into selection for teaching; suggestions for regular staff appraisal of teachers, and the public reporting by Her Majesty's Inspectorate of their findings on visits to schools and colleges.

Developments in Scotland

Scotland is a compact educational entity with long experience of strongly centralised modes of operation. The effectiveness of these centralised procedures is demonstrated in the management of the major programme of changes in curriculum and assessment currently taking place in Scotland.

Two national committees were established in 1974, one by the Consultative Committee on the Curriculum, the nominated body responsible for advising the Secretary of State on curriculum matters, to examine the structure of the curriculum for 14–16 year-olds (the Munn Committee) and the other by the Secretary of State himself to consider assessment at 16+ (the Dunning Committee). Both committees reported in 1977. Munn advocated a core plus options curriculum pattern, which required pupils to undertake work in each of eight 'modes of activity' as follows:

linguistic/literary
mathematics
social studies
scientific

religious education
moral education
aesthetic studies
physical education.

Dunning recommended a complex pattern of 'assessment for all', covering the whole age range and enabling pupils to reach one of three levels of achievement – merit, general or foundation – in each area of study. Following extensive feasibility studies into timetabling arrangements and the technical aspects of the assessment proposals, the Secretary of State produced his response to the reports in 1980. He considered that the eight modes of study proposed by the Munn Committee 'provide a curriculum framework which all schools should adopt'. He also intimated that the assessment proposals would be implemented. After further piloting of appropriate curriculum and assessment materials, the Secretary of State intimated in 1982 that there would be a phased implementation of the proposals, beginning in August 1984. That decision called for the setting up of joint working parties, for each of the subject areas, with responsibility for devising guidelines for the new syllabuses and specifying the detailed criteria relating to their assessment. The activities of these joint working parties have been intensive and will continue for some years until all the syllabus and assessment arrangements have been completed for all the subjects that will feature in the new Standard Grade assessments at 16+.

In all of this work the Department has taken the lead and has orchestrated what is, by any standards, a massive programme of development work with remarkable energy and determination. In the process it has, if anything, reinforced the central control which the SED exerts over the work of the schools in Scotland.

Technical and Vocational Education Initiative (TVEI)

In November 1982 the Prime Minister announced the government's intention to launch TVEI, a five-year project to be conducted by the Manpower Services Commission 'to explore and test methods of organising, managing and resourcing replicable programmes of general, technical and vocational education' for young people between the ages of 14 and 18. This initiative was designed to stimulate local authorities to mount full-time programmes which would be funded from central funds – to the extent of £400,000 per project – provided that they met certain centrally determined criteria. These criteria were as follows:

1   Equal opportunities should be available to young people of both sexes and they should normally be educated together on courses within each project. Care should be taken to avoid sex stereotyping.

2   Programmes should provide 4-year curricula with progression from year to year, designed to prepare the student for particular aspects of employment and for adult life in a society liable to rapid change.

3   Programmes should have clear and specific objectives, including the objectives of encouraging initiative, problem-solving abilities, and other aspects of personal development.

4   The balance between the general, technical and vocational elements of programmes should vary according to students' individual needs and the stage of the course, but throughout the programme there should be both a general and a technical/vocational element.

5   The technical and vocational elements should be broadly related to potential employment opportunities within and outside the geographical area for the young people concerned.

6   There should be appropriate planned work experience as an integral part of the programme from the age of 15 onwards.

7   Courses offered should be capable of being linked effectively with subsequent training/educational opportunities.

8   Arrangements should be made for regular assessment and for students and tutors to discuss students' performance/progress.[16]

Projects in Scotland had, in addition, to demonstrate their compatibility with national curriculum development initiatives for 14–16 year-olds and 16–18 year-olds.

   In the first year of its operation TVEI sponsored 14 projects; in its second year a further 48 projects were mounted, including 5 in

Scotland. In 1985 a further 11 programmes were introduced in England and Wales and one more in Scotland.

While the schemes are voluntary, in the sense that LEAs are not obliged to mount them and pupils are not compulsorily involved, and while the programmes demonstrate the variety that is to be expected from vigorous local initiatives, the significance of TVEI is unmistakable. As the responsibility of the Department of Employment, TVEI represents a determined government effort, practically by-passing the government department that has traditionally exercised responsibility for the schools and the school curriculum, to effect a swift and decisive orientation of the curriculum towards what is considered to be of immediate relevance to the skills and know-how required by a technological society.

Conclusion

The evidence adduced in this chapter undeniably points to the development over the past decade of increased government involvement in curriculum matters. On both sides of the border the central authority has asserted itself, not through the open interventionist strategy of prescribing what pupils should learn, but by progressively exerting pressure on LEAs to ensure that in their schools all pupils were exposed to a central core of learnings up to age 16. At the same time, there were other developments, themselves instigated by central government, which had the effect of strengthening the influence of central government on the curriculum. Why, then, was it considered necessary for central government to strengthen its influence on the shape of the school curriculum? What were the factors that were thought to justify the institution of a national curriculum framework? The issues raised by these questions are explored in the next chapter.

References

1 Dennis Lawton (1980) *The Politics of the School Curriculum*, pp. 15–16. London: Routledge and Kegan Paul.
2 Sir Keith Joseph, speech to North of England Education Conference, Sheffield, as reported in *Times Educational Supplement*, 13 January 1984.
3 James Callaghan, 'Towards a National Debate', speech at Ruskin College, October 1976, as reported in *Education*, 22 October 1976.
4 Quoted in Tim Devlin and Mary Warnock (1977) *What must we teach?* London: Temple Smith.

5 Quoted in Tim Devlin and Mary Warnock (1977) *What must we teach?*, p. 11. London: Temple Smith.
6 Maurice Holt (1983) *Curriculum Workshop: An Introduction to Whole Curriculum Planning*, p. 21. London: Routledge and Kegan Paul.
7 Department of Education and Science/Welsh Office (1979) *Local Authority Arrangements for the School Curriculum*, Report on the Circular 14.77 Review. London: HMSO.
8 Department of Education and Science (1984) *English from 5–16*. London: HMSO.
9 Department of Education and Science (1985) *Science 5–16: A Statement of Policy*. London: HMSO.
10 *The Sunday Times*, 31 March 1985, p. 17.
11 Department of Education and Science (1985) *Better Schools*. London: HMSO.
12 The Schools Council (1975) Working Paper 53, *The Whole Curriculum 13–16*. London: Evans/Methuen Educational.
13 *Hansard*, 22 April 1982.
14 Malcolm Skilbeck (1984) 'Curriculum Evaluation at the National Level' in Malcolm Skilbeck (ed.) *Evaluating the Curriculum in the Eighties*. London: Hodder and Stoughton.
15 Jean Dawson (1984) 'The Work of the Assessment of Performance Unit' in Malcolm Skilbeck (ed.) *Evaluating the Curriculum in the Eighties*. London: Hodder and Stoughton.
16 *TVEI Review 1984* (1984). London: Manpower Services Commission.

2

The Case for a Core Curriculum

The term 'core curriculum' suggests that, whatever learning experiences pupils undertake, there are certain essential activities at the heart of their programme of studies. The core curriculum will constitute those activities or studies that all pupils will be expected to undertake. The term also implies that the core will constitute only part of pupils' total programme. Clearly, it is possible to conceive of a variety of different core curricula in different schools. What school A takes to constitute a core of essential learnings may well differ from what is thought to be essential by school B. However, the notion of a core curriculum that is developed on a national basis – that was the focus of the discussion in Chapter 1 – implies a measure of agreement nationally about the nature and composition of the core. In some countries what pupils are expected to learn is elaborated in very considerable detail by central government agencies and schools are obliged to conform to the national prescription. As was noted in Chapter 1, that kind of central control over syllabus content is anathema in Britain. What is sought is an agreed framework for the curriculum. In a democratic society the institution of a nationally agreed curriculum framework, however impressively it may be articulated, is unlikely to be effected simply by government edict; it will need to be the product of consultation and to be a response to a good deal of professional, as well as public, discussion of the issues involved. This chapter seeks to elucidate the arguments and considerations which underpin the case for a national core curriculum. No claim is made that these arguments directly brought about the ministerial initiatives described in Chapter 1. However, they undoubtedly formed part of that public and professional discussion to which the ministerial initiatives were the response and in relation to which the credibility and plausibility of these initiatives must be judged. The arguments are grouped under the following headings:

Standards in the Curriculum
The Curriculum and its Relevance to Adult Life
The Curriculum and the Democratic Community
The Curriculum and the Nature of Knowledge
The Curriculum and Accountability
International Comparisons
The Creation of Coherence in the Curriculum.

Standards in the Curriculum

The decade of the 1960s witnessed significant changes in education. Progressive or informal approaches were officially endorsed in the Plowden Report of 1967.[1] That report set out the assumptions on which progressive education was based:

The child is the agent of his own learning . . . Activity and experience, both physical and mental, are often the best means of gaining knowledge and acquiring facts . . . Facts are best retained when they are used and understood, when right attitudes to learning are created, when children learn to learn. (Para. 5.29)

Skills of reading writing, or the techniques used in art and craft, can best be taught when the need for these is evident to children. (Para. 5.30)

The corresponding Scottish document, which appeared in 1965, encapsulated the new philosophy in these words:

The primary school child has a natural curiosity and a desire to learn which makes him capable of seriously and deliberately pursuing his own education on lines of his own choice. He needs, and should be given, opportunities to explore and investigate his environment, to make his own discoveries and draw his own conclusions, to observe, to experiment, to collect, to construct, to read and to record . . . His ability to express himself and to communicate with others can only be hampered by the imposition in the classroom of an unnatural silence and by a too-early insistence on conventional correctness.[2]

The official endorsement of progressive approaches to primary education was accompanied by the ending of selection at 11 or 12 and by the introduction of comprehensive schools where, in the early years at least, pupils were taught in mixed-ability groups. These changes were not always met with enthusiasm, even within the teaching profession. Selection at the end of primary schooling had been defended by many as a way of defining standards in the basic skills that should be attained by primary school pupils. In the late '60s and early '70s the volume of criticism was very considerably increased. Indeed, criticism was on occasions so strident and the public debate so intense and protracted as to indicate widespread disquiet about whether these educational changes really constituted improvements. There were three factors that were themselves symptomatic of the prevailing concern at the same time as they served to inflame it.

The first of these was the publication between 1969 and 1977 of five documents known as the *Black Papers* on education. Each of these was a collection of articles and anecdotes written by academics, teachers and others, and each amounted to a sustained and withering denunciation of current educational practices. With full debunking fervour they attacked informal and progressive approaches in the primary school, the end of selection at 11+, the teaching of pupils in mixed-ability groups, the extension of comprehensive schooling at the expense of grammar and other types of secondary school, and the changes taking place in higher education in response to student unrest. Their central thesis was that these developments together constituted a most serious threat to traditional educational values, which they held to be the ordered initiation of the young through disciplined study and formal competitive examination into the cultural and scientific heritage, and the 'great achievements of past civilisation'. That conception of education, it was maintained, appeared everywhere to be under attack; standards were on the decline; *laissez-faire* approaches in the primary school permitted children to do as they pleased; too many teachers were incompetent; conventional notions of discipline and hard work were treated with contempt; and truancy, indiscipline and violence were to be encountered on a massive and growing scale. In their intense advocacy the Black Papers had more in common with traditional pamphleteering than with scholarly debate and that was reflected in some cases in a mode of presentation that was evocative of educational mayhem and in language that seemed to herald a new dark age – 'Moving Progressively Backwards', 'Comprehensive Disaster', 'The Rise of Mediocracy', 'Decline and Fall of the University Idea', 'The Enterprise is Sick'. The very title of the series – Black Papers – inviting, as it did, the comparison with official Green Papers and White Papers on education, stressed the severity of the country's educational ills and the bleakness of the outlook.

The Black Papers certainly provoked widespread public discussion and their supporters might well have deduced that the public reaction demonstrated that the Black Papers reflected public concern. Teachers and others involved in education reacted to the Black Papers less favourably. The Minister for Education of the day, Mr Short, told the House of Commons that the publication of the first Black Paper marked 'the blackest day in educational history for 100 years'. In a study of the Black Papers, in which there is a careful examination of the ways in which the Black Paper authors misinterpreted and misrepresented the findings of several major research studies, it was concluded that:

> The unfortunate thing is that many people who do not have the time or inclination to study these reports for themselves will have assumed, since many prominent names are associated with the Black Papers, that the accounts given there of these researches are fair and accurate. In this sense, the Black Papers have made a major contribution to public ignorance.[3]

Whether or not that judgement is valid, it is undeniably the case that the appearance of the Black Papers and the reception they received indicated a strong degree of public concern about the work of the schools and the quality of their pupils' achievements.

The second factor which highlighted public concern about schooling was the case of the William Tyndale Junior School in Islington, London, which erupted in 1975. At one level, the troubles of the school arose from a clash of educational philosophies. Most of the teachers in the school, invoking the progressivism of Plowden, sought to instil in pupils the responsibility for their own learning. In the difficult circumstances of the inner city they had abandoned the attempt to teach children the basic skills in a conventional way; they had rejected coercion of any kind, and sought to create an altogether freer and more flexible environment in which pupils would learn at their own pace and in their own time. Some of the parents and managers of the school did not share that interpretation of events. They had heard the headteacher claim that the skill of writing did not matter any longer; they knew that a teacher had written 'I hate reading groups' on the blackboard and sent the children out to play; they had received reports of children being left to watch television and enjoy long hours of ping-pong; they had evidence of violent and disruptive behaviour on the part of pupils; and they strongly suspected that there were teachers in the school who were using their professional position for political purposes. In short, for such parents and managers, William Tyndale was the antithesis of a school and had become a disreputable shambles.

There developed a sustained conflict between teachers and managers, each accusing the other of harbouring political motives, until the school disintegrated and a public enquiry was conducted on the whole affair.[4] While the case raised many questions about the control of the curriculum and the accountability of teachers and of managers, there is no doubt that the sustained exposure which the affairs of the school attracted reinforced in the public mind the suspicion that all was not well with the schools.

The third factor was the publication in 1976 of a major study on the effectiveness of different teaching approaches carried out at Lancaster University by Neville Bennett.[5] The study compared the performance of the pupils in three different types of teaching environment:

Informal   Those teachers whose classroom work was in line with the progressive philosophy of Plowden;

Formal   Those teachers whose classroom work was in line with traditional practice;

Mixed   Those teachers whose classroom work included informal as well as formal characteristics.

The pupils of these different groups of teachers were tested on a variety of measures. The analysis of the results demonstrated the superiority of the 'formal' methods of teaching with regard to pupils' achievements in reading, in Mathematics and in English. Besides, pupils taught by 'formal' teachers were as good at creative or imaginative work as their peers who were taught by 'informal' teachers. While this study was the focus of considerable controversy in educational circles and among those professionally involved in educational research, it was interpreted by the wider community as demonstrating the ill-effects of the widespread adoption of progressive and informal methods, despite the evidence of the researchers that only about 17% of schools had adopted informal methods, and as confirming the need for a return to a form of schooling which paid due regard to achievement in the basic skills. At the same time, opposition was expressed in those areas where local education authority policy favoured informal methods and where, therefore, the report was interpreted as critical of LEA policy.

The Black Papers, the William Tyndale case, and the research study on teaching styles, all seemed to focus public attention on the nature of the standards schools might be expected to maintain and on the extent to which they were indeed maintaining them. Contributors to the Great Debate helped to swell the chorus of criticism at the low achievements of school leavers in the basic skills. Several representatives from industry testified that alarming proportions of would-be apprentices disqualified themselves by their incapacity to perform simple reading and computational tasks satisfactorily. The Director of Army Education reported that three-quarters of the 43,000 applicants for the Army had to be turned down on educational grounds.[6] At a different level, universities and other institutions of higher education bemoaned the number of students – the so-called successes of the school system – who were incapable of spelling accurately or writing in sentences. Finally, the fact that something like 100,000 people a year were receiving help from the Adult Literacy Campaign was taken to be further evidence of the failure of the schools.

The public debate focused on whether or not standards were declining. It was frequently maintained that like was not being compared with like: for example, those who 20 years previously had entered apprenticeships were now staying on at school and entering higher education. The more productive line of discussion accepted that, whether or not standards were declining, they were not high enough and had failed to keep up with the rise in expectations about what life in contemporary society requires. If that, indeed, was the case, and in view of the increasing public investment in education, the remedy might well lie in bringing the priorities in the school curriculum under closer public control.

The Curriculum and its Relevance to Adult Life

Public concern was also expressed about the relevance of the school curriculum. In this connection, there were two main criticisms. On the one hand, it was maintained that the curriculum was divorced from the social realities of pupils' experience and failed to equip them with the skills and understanding necessary for survival in the contemporary world. The curriculum, the argument went, was preoccupied with 'academic' rather than 'action' knowledge, of the kind that enabled a person to cope with the increased range of choices and demands imposed by contemporary social life. On this view, there was a dissociation between the content of the various disciplines of the school curriculum and the central concerns of young people. Indeed, this dissociation was so pronounced that education for very many became a boring ritual that quite failed to speak to their condition.

Various attempts had been made to counter the heavily academic orientation of the school curriculum – for example, by the introduction of guidance systems, social education programmes, and other activities that were geared to the realisation of more explicitly social objectives. However, these had been ascribed a merely marginal status and could not begin to compete for curricular time with established academic activities, not even in response to those critics who pointed to the growing incidence of alcoholism, drug abuse, vandalism, delinquency, marital and psychological breakdown, and who sought to establish a connection between such indications of social malaise and deficiencies in the school curriculum. Indeed, if anything, the introduction of guidance and social education activities could be interpreted by teachers to strengthen the academic orientation of their work, on the assumption that, with the introduction of social education staff, they had been exonerated from the responsibility of relating their teaching to the business of living and growing up in a complex society.

The concern that the curriculum should nurture the pupils' social and personal development was matched by a conviction that the curriculum ill-prepared pupils for life in an industrial society. Of course, there had been a long-standing aversion to regarding schools as the proper locus for vocational training: their function was broader, reflecting the fact that work related to only one of the roles of adult life. However, critics maintained, it is one thing to avoid a narrow vocationalism: it is quite another to fail to induct pupils into the industrial and technological aspects of contemporary life and to equip them with skills upon which subsequent technological training can be based. Representatives of the world of industry and commerce strongly suspected that the schools diverted pupils from the world of technology, partly out of a totally erroneous belief that technology did not offer the same intellectual challenge as traditional academic studies, and partly in response to the deeply entrenched prejudice in society at large that the 'doing' and 'making' of which technology consists were unworthy activities for an educated person to profess. Critics insisted that a curriculum which neglected this important area was as deficient as a curriculum which devoted insufficient attention to social and personal development. Nor was there any need to choose between such claims: both were considered to have a legitimate place in the school curriculum and measures were perhaps required to ensure that such claims were fully recognised.

The Curriculum and the Democratic Community

The criticisms of the school curriculum that have just been considered imply that there is a relationship between education and social life. Indeed, a powerful tradition of educational thinking maintains that the content of the curriculum, and its justification, derives from an examination of what is required for effective participation in the way of life of the community. The school curriculum is taken to constitute a set of publicly agreed learnings and to provide a common educational experience shared by all members of the community. There are four identifiable strands in this tradition.

The first was espoused by the advocates of comprehensive education. They maintained that the necessary consequence of the reorganisation of schools along comprehensive lines was the institution of a comprehensive curriculum. Such a curriculum would provide all pupils with access to the same range of learning experiences: it would terminate the 'educational apartheid' of providing some pupils with an academically demanding programme that paved the way to extended education, while others underwent a truncated programme that was organised on radically different principles; and it would correct the curricular imbalances which allowed some pupils to pursue intellectual objectives at the expense, for example, of social and personal development, and vice versa. A common curriculum was defended as the means by which society ensured that all its children received the kind of education that was theirs by right and all its citizens were brought to certain minimum levels of understanding and achievement. In this way, the potential of all pupils would be developed for the benefit of the individual pupils themselves and of society, which depended for its survival on the cultivation of the talents and skills of everyone. It was felt that by instituting a curriculum of this kind full equality of educational opportunity would be realised. Moreover, by ensuring that all pupils underwent together a common experience of schooling, there might be an end to social divisiveness and class distinctions. The social cohesiveness upon which democracy was based required a common curriculum.

The second strand in this tradition maintained that the path to a common culture was through a common curriculum and sought to identify the ingredients of a common culture as the basis of curriculum planning. Dennis Lawton, in one example of this approach, asserts that the curriculum represents a 'selection from the culture'.[7] The selection from the culture is derived by undertaking a 'cultural analysis' of a given society, an analysis of its different institutions and of the principles informing its whole mode of operation. Such an analysis suggests that a society consists of a number of 'systems' as follows:

1   Social Structure/Social System
2   Economic System
3   Communication System
4   Rationality System
5   Technology System

6   Morality System
7   Belief System
8   Aesthetic System.

The curriculum is derived by making adequate selections from each of these eight 'systems'. That is, the school curriculum will involve pupils in the development of skill and understanding relating to each of eight dimensions of social life. It is envisaged that teachers, possibly from different subject areas, will cooperate in the devising of syllabuses for each of these areas. For example, the technological dimension might be developed by teachers in craft, design and technology, home economics and computer studies; and the aesthetic system might be attended to by developing a coherent programme drawn from art, drama, film and TV studies. The result would be a common curriculum which equipped pupils with the capacity to undertake and participate fully in the life of the community.

A third approach, advanced by David Hargreaves,[8] has sought to establish a direct connection between the notion of community and the school curriculum. This view holds that a good society is one in which human beings achieve dignity through involvement in various forms of community life and corporate experience. While community life has been eroded through, for example, the disintegration of traditional communities and the cultivation of individualism, it can be regenerated through an appropriately modified school curriculum. It is proposed that all secondary schools should have 'a central core curriculum which would be organised round community studies and the expressive arts': it would take up approximately half of the curriculum and would be a compulsory curriculum 'for all pupils of whatever abilities and social backgrounds'. Such a curriculum would, of course, involve pupils in various forms of community activity; it would engage them in the analysis of different communities, of family life, of institutional structures, of the distribution of power; and it would seek to equip pupils with the skills required for effective participation in community life. The emphasis given to the expressive arts in the proposed core has a two-fold justification: on the one hand, they themselves are a powerful means of generating corporate activity; in the second place, the combination of community studies and expressive arts will challenge the dominant position which 'intellectual/cognitive' activities have enjoyed and allow greater attention to be devoted to activities which promote 'aesthetic/artistic', 'affective/emotional', 'physical/manual', and 'personal/social' development.

Finally, arguments have been advanced to show that the principles embedded in the notion of democracy itself point to the need for a core curriculum. Democracy, it is claimed, involves a commitment to certain basic principles including rationality, fairness, tolerance, respect for others, and truth. In turn, it is maintained that pupils who are being initiated into a democratic way of life need to acquire a very extensive range of dispositions that derive directly from a commitment to democratic principles. For example, they must become disposed to behaving rationally, to refuse to accept claims without appropriate evidence, to have a questioning attitude to authority, to settle disputes through persuasion, to be prepared to work things out for themselves, and much else besides. What is more, the commitment to democratic principles is impossible without a very extensive range of understandings: it calls for a knowledge of one's own situation, of the economic and political context, of factors relating to one's professional activities, of what makes other people tick, of alternative lifestyles, of leisure activities, of why there are disagreements on a whole range of social and moral issues, and a host of other matters. If, then, as is frequently urged, schools are concerned to induct pupils into a democratic way of life there is a pressing necessity for a curriculum which fosters the dispositions, the skills and knowledge which a commitment to democracy requires.

In their different ways these arguments point to the need for the institution of certain essential elements in the curriculum as a way of preparing pupils for participating fully in a democratic society.

The Curriculum and the Nature of Knowledge

Among the most influential arguments in the case for a core curriculum were those advanced by philosophers of education on the basis of their analysis of the nature of knowledge. The central thrust of such arguments was that human knowledge and understanding has become progressively differentiated into a number of categories or 'forms'. Each of these employs its own concepts, its own characteristic mode of enquiry and investigation, and its own means of distinguishing between true and false, good and bad, right and wrong. Together, these different forms of knowledge constitute the available ways of understanding and interpreting human experience and the only ways in which such understanding can be extended. Here, then, was a thesis that negated the claim that 'all knowledge is one' and that the differences between the disciplines were 'arbitrary' or 'artificial'. On the contrary, physical science, for example, was a distinctively different kind of discipline from mathematics, and both of these were radically different from the study of literature or music. The differences were far from arbitrary: they reflected basic differences in the way in which the concepts were interrelated, and the analytical and investigative procedures deployed.

In the argument put forward, Paul Hirst has concluded that human knowledge is reducible to the following seven forms:

logic and mathematics
physical sciences
'awareness of our own and other people's minds'
ethics
aesthetics
religion
philosophy[9]

In effect, each of the forms consisted of a family of disciplines, with each member deriving its family resemblance from the fact that it shared a distinctive methodology and mode of rational activity. Of course, in each of the forms knowledge had been progressively accumulated through the work of its constituent disciplines. However, the forms were not to be seen merely as stocks of accumulated knowledge: they each constituted a tradition of intellectual enquiry, a means whereby knowledge was developed, and in coming to terms with a form of knowledge it was necessary to master its apparatus for generating knowledge.

The curricular implications of such a thesis were clear: if each of the forms was distinctive, if each was a means of structuring human experience, then schools should make provision for pupils to be systematically initiated into all of them. The curriculum should engage all pupils in the study of exemplars of each of the forms of knowledge. A curriculum so constructed would equip pupils with what were called 'the tools of autonomy', the conceptual apparatus necessary for the making of judgements about, and making sense of, human experience. Since it constituted in contemporary terms the intellectual equipment of the educated person it had to be the birthright of every pupil.

For curriculum planners, the forms of knowledge philosophy provided the framework they were seeking. While there were some who disputed that all forms of knowledge could be reduced to seven 'forms', that philosophy was seized upon as an effective means of ordering what had become, through the proliferation of new subjects and the need to accommodate new demands, an over-crowded curriculum; it provided the answer to those who had been searching for the 'essentials' of education or for a 'balanced' curriculum; and it was the antidote to premature specialisation and the haphazardness of a curriculum that was being dominated by options.

The forms of knowledge thesis had a variety of different manifestations: 'realms of meaning'; 'modes of activity'; 'areas of experience'; 'ways of knowing'. Most of these, including the eight 'sytems' of cultural analysis discussed earlier, were clearly derived from the original forms of knowledge thesis and were used to reduce an extensive range of different subjects and disciplines into a limited number of distinctive categories which might provide a framework for the school curriculum. However, one related thesis was developed in a highly novel way by John White and is worth highlighting in the present context, particularly since it was elaborated in a book whic¹ bore the title *Towards a Compulsory Curriculum*.[10] White begins by acknowledging that to require children to attend school for eleven years constitutes a fairly devastating encroachment on their liberty. Can such a constraint on pupils' freedom be justified? White maintains that education should help pupils to choose for themselves the kind of lives they wish to lead and the sort of activities they wish to pursue. The rational exercise of choice, however, implies an understanding of as many activities and ways of life as possible. At this point, White introduces two categories of activity:

category (i)   activities which cannot be understood without being engaged in;

category (ii) activities which can be at least partly understood without being engaged in.

The distinction is illustrated by comparing linguistic communication and climbing mountains. The first is an example of a category (i) activity, because one cannot understand what it is to communicate unless one actually communicates; whereas climbing mountains is an example of a category (ii) activity because one can understand something of what is involved, for example, by watching a film on the ascent of Everest. White claims, in this argument, that category (i) activities should constitute a core of compulsory studies for pupils in school. These would be communication, mathematics, physical sciences, appreciating works of art, philosophy, history, and social studies. All of these are activities which pupils should be required to engage in if they are to understand them and subsequently make decisions about which activities they wish to follow and which forms of life they wish to pursue. That is the justification for interfering with the pupils' liberty: their freedom is restricted at one point in time to enable them to exercise freedom subsequently. Of course, White maintains, the curriculum may consist of all kinds of other activities but these would be voluntary. The compulsory activities would be those listed, a list that is not too dissimilar from the forms of knowledge earlier mentioned. *Towards a Compulsory Curriculum* was seen by its author as an attempt to initiate the public discussion of a national common curriculum, and as a thesis that might have been of interest to politicians and others. Apparently, the only politician who appeared to react favourably to the case and to communicate with the author was Sir Keith Joseph.

The Curriculum and Accountability

The notion of accountability in education is a complex one. It concerns the whole network of relationships involving teachers, pupils, parents, local education authorities, central government, and the public. In the present context the term refers to the growing demand that teachers should be more openly accountable in the sense that they should be expected to meet clearly defined expectations. There were two related factors that influenced the growth of demands of this kind. In the first place, in times of fiscal stringency, to which people in Britain have become increasingly accustomed, and when the available funds must be allocated only after the most careful scrutiny of priorities, the work of the schools is bound to be open to closer inspection and questions are bound to be raised about whether value is being obtained for money. The massive public investment in education has led almost inevitably to a demand for evidence of the effectiveness of the investment.

In the second place, publicity given to the debate on standards, the Black Papers, the William Tyndale case, and other matters, raised the issue of whether teachers were meeting the obligations expected of them. In the light of such evidence, the demand for increased public control of the curriculum and for a clear specification of what might be expected of the schools became more plausible. Of course, that demand called for a readjustment to the conventional understanding of where responsibility for curricular matters was vested. Over the years, teachers had responded to the relative passivity of central and local government on curricular matters and had assumed responsibility for what pupils were taught and resolutely defended their entitlement to carry that responsibility. Nevertheless, partly in response to the Black Papers and the concern about standards, support grew for a greater public say in the shape of the curriculum. It was maintained that the school curriculum was closely related to the country's future and, as such, was clearly a matter of public policy. Teachers might very well have clearly defined professional responsibilities with regard to the best ways of promoting learning – that is to say with regard to the *means* of education – but that did not entitle them, as teachers, to be sole authorities on the *ends* of education. These ends should surely be the product of public discussion and debate and should ultimately be determined not by a professional body of teachers, but by a body representative of public opinion in general. The argument has been summarised, by Paul Hirst, in these words:

> The professionals' understanding in detail of what might be achieved in schools and how it is best pursued does not exhaust the considerations relevant to deciding what pupils should, indeed, learn. The very considerable long-term significance of that learning for both the individual and society introduces matters quite beyond the expertise not only of teachers but of all other

professionals within the educational service. To decisions about the organisation and resourcing of the maintained school system, professionals with varying roles within the educational service can bring crucial knowledge. But the wider implications of the decisions mean that other professionals and the public at large have interests that must be taken into account. Professionals are not experts on what is the general good that education should serve, nor on which more particular ends it should serve in a number of controversial areas, nor on important aspects of educational organisation and the allocation of resources. These other considerations are primarily matters of public policy.[11]

Views of that kind pointed to the need for the accountability of teachers to be made explicit: they would need to accept the obligation to pursue aims that had been determined by the community.

International Comparisons

The way a country arranges its educational provision is clearly influenced by, and reflects, broader social values and assumptions and cannot be invalidated by demonstrating that its arrangements do not obtain elsewhere. At the same time, it is as well to note that tribal customs are not laws of nature; the fact that educational systems vary is an invitation to consider whether any given set of arrangements might be modified.

The striking feature of educational provision in other countries is the strong degree of central control over the curriculum. Not only is it common to find a nationally agreed framework for the curriculum with time allocations for particular components, but this can also be accompanied by very detailed specifications governing aims, teaching/learning strategies, and textbooks. Such 'state-controlled' curricula – a notion which excites such deep suspicions and hostility in Britain – are to be found not only in countries in the eastern bloc but also in France and the Scandinavian countries. In all of these countries curricular provision is seen as part of a wider programme of social action and a means of creating the educated society. Indeed, in such countries it would be considered odd that such an important issue as what is taught in schools should be left undefined and inderterminate. What, in Britain, might be regarded as evidence of freedom and local diversity would, for them, be evidence of government irresponsibility.

The Creation of Coherence in the Curriculum

The final set of considerations that might be adduced in support of the case for a core curriculum relate to the growing conviction that curricular provision had become incoherent and uncoordinated. That incoherence manifested itself in many ways. There were discontinuities between primary schools and secondary schools. Indeed, there was no machinery for ensuring that a pupil's curriculum constituted a coherent and progressive educational experience. Schools took pride in their own system of options but these were frequently based on staffing availability rather than on educational principle and commonly allowed pupils to discontinue study in such key areas as science. The haphazardness created by such option schemes with all their eccentricities was aggravated by the plethora (in England and Wales, at any rate) of examining bodies and of the curricular schemes they each generated. There were twenty separate examination boards, each awarding its own certificate, many hundreds of subject titles and nearly 19,000 different syllabuses. While the external examination system had been regarded as a means of maintaining a degree of control over the curriculum, since 1964, CSE (Mode 3), had vested very considerable responsibility in individual schools for curriculum and assessment. The greater freedom granted to teachers by such a move could be interpreted as an impetus to institutional creativity or, less favourably, as a further lurch to disorder. The prevailing diversity and variety of curricular provision was thought to be educationally disruptive, particularly for the geographically mobile. Their children were the ones, it was claimed, who were liable to encounter 'Dinosaurs' or 'The Vikings' three or four times during their primary schooling and whose secondary education was very seriously dislocated by the variety of option schemes and syllabuses.

There were other factors that accentuated the sense of curricular instability. The years in question were characterised by widespread curriculum development and experimentation. While many would regard such curricular revitalisation as an educational necessity there were others who regarded it as little more than dabbling in the specious and the mounting of bandwagons. Worse still, the writings of the 'deschoolers' and the 'free schoolers', not least through the polemical thrust of their titles – *School is Dead, Deschooling Society, Teaching as a Subversive Activity, Compulsory Miseducation* – seemed to herald educational anarchy and to constitute a further destabilising influence.

Faced with many changes and the prospect of even more radical change, many yearned for a period of curricular consolidation, if not a return to the status quo ante. In such circumstances there was support for those who stressed the need to establish agreement on what eleven years of compulsory education were intended to constitute, and who thought that aim was realisable through the introduction of a national core curriculum.

Conclusion

This chapter has sought to draw together from a variety of different sources the arguments advanced for a national curriculum framework or a core of essential learnings for all pupils. In their different ways, these arguments reflected dissatisfaction with existing curricular arrangements. The curriculum was considered to be failing to maintain standards; to be unrelated to the requirements of society in general and of a democratic society in particular; to take insufficient account of the ways in which distinctive types of knowledge contributed to pupils' intellectual and social development; to be subject to the irregularities of option schemes; to be too strongly under the influence of individual schools and teachers; and to fail to reflect a national consensus on what pupils should learn. The most appropriate response to all of these supposed shortcomings in the curriculum was thought to be the introduction of a national curriculum framework which embodied public expectations of what pupils should learn and schools should teach.

1 Plowden Report (1967) *Children and their Primary Schools*. London: HMSO.
2 Scottish Education Department (1965) *Primary Education in Scotland*. Edinburgh: HMSO.
3 Nigel Wright (1977) *Progress in Education*. London: Croom Helm.
4 R. Auld (1976) *William Tyndale Junior and Infant Schools Public Enquiry*. London: Inner London Education Authority.
5 N. Bennett (1976) *Teaching Styles and Pupil Progress*. London: Open Books.

6 Reported in Tim Devlin and Mary Warnock (1977) *What must we teach?* London: Temple Smith.

7 Denis Lawton (1983) *Curriculum Studies and Educational Planning*. London: Hodder and Stoughton.

8 David H. Hargreaves (1982) *The Challenge for the Comprehensive School*. London: Routledge and Kegan Paul.

9 P. Hirst and R. S. Peters (1970) *The Logic of Education*. London: Routledge and Kegan Paul.

10 John White (1973) *Towards a Compulsory Curriculum*. London: Routledge and Kegan Paul.

11 P. Hirst (1972) 'Professional Authority: Its Foundations and Limits', *British Journal of Educational Studies*, Vol. XXX, No. 2, pp. 172–182.

3

The Core Curriculum and its Critics

Introduction

Educational activity is controversial in the sense that people dis-
agree about its ends and about how these ends should be realised.
These disagreements are most evident in discussions about the
content of the curriculum. Inevitably, then, the case for a core
curriculum has been met by a considerable body of public and
professional criticism. This chapter seeks to elucidate the most
significant of these counter arguments. It will focus on six main lines
of attack and will seek to establish in each case the extent to which
the thrust of the argument invalidates the notion of a national
curriculum framework. That analysis will pave the way for a reconciliation between the notion of such a curriculum framework and
the reservations that have been expressed about it. The six lines of
criticism will, for convenience, be referred to as six theses. These
theses relate to:

1 pupil choice
2 differentiation
3 the impossibility of consensus
4 cultural pluralism
5 the decentralisation of power
6 the professional autonomy of teachers

It is emphasised that these are not to be regarded as discrete lines of
criticism. As will be seen, the various arguments interrelate at
several points. However, each thesis constitutes such a significant
and substantial critique of a national curriculum framework that it
justifies a separate analysis.

Thesis 1: Pupil Choice

The proponents of thesis 1 maintain that the overriding principle of curriculum planning relates not to the nature of knowledge or to the needs of society but to pupil choice. It is insisted that pupils have a right to select those curricular activities which accord with their vocational aspirations or personal inclinations. The advantages of involvement in curricular activities in which pupils have a deep and continuing interest are thought to be self-evident. The key to the curricular problem is thought to lie, therefore, not in extending the range of compulsory activities in the hope that pupils' weaknesses may thereby be eliminated, but in creating maximum scope for pupil choice and in this way allowing pupils to cultivate their strengths through intensive study of activities they find interesting. From this point of view, indeed, the whole point of education is to enable pupils to pursue with deeper sophistication, insight and understanding, the activities which *they* value. Failure to recognise this principle is thought to explain the deep malaise in contemporary secondary education. The fundamental problem facing the secondary schools is considered to be the motivational problem: many, if not most, pupils are ill-disposed to engage in a curriculum that consists, for the most part, of activities that are valued not by the pupils themselves but by teachers and by the adult community. Teachers may strive to make such a curriculum interesting but such attempts result in a kind of forced feeding. In consequence, many pupils find themselves at best being manipulated and at worst totally alienated. On this analysis, the problem of motivation is one that is created by teachers themselves: they persist in seeking to initiate pupils into activities that are of no interest to them. The establishment of a national core curriculum, it is claimed, will therefore exacerbate what is widely acknowledged already to be an extremely serious problem.

The principle of pupil choice is defended on moral as well as on psychological grounds. It is maintained that the overriding aim of education is the development of autonomy – the cultivation of those capacities for independent decision-making associated with the self-regulating moral agent. In keeping with that educational aim, practices should be adopted which strengthen pupils' dispositions to behave autonomously – to make choices, to work things out for themselves, and so on. Such a disposition is thought to be strengthened by allowing pupils to choose their own curricular objectives, to pursue whichever curricular activities they wish, and in other ways to assume full responsibility for their own learning. By contrast, the argument runs, the conventional relationship between teachers and pupils is an authoritarian and exploitative one: pupils are required to study traditions of knowledge that reflect the teachers' value system and to pursue arbitrarily selected objectives which do not command the pupils' consent. Such an education, far from liberating pupils, prolongs their domination by adults, enslaves them to orthodox modes of thinking and action that are imposed and therefore alien, and frustrates the emergence of the truly autonomous person. The introduction of a compulsory core curriculum would, on this analysis, be morally offensive.

The watch-words of thesis 1, then, are 'choice', 'interest', and 'autonomy'. It is evocative of progressive and radical traditions in education which emphasise the diversity and flexibility of curricular provision now associated with 'open learning'. Such 'open learning' systems – and, of course, they need not be confined to schools – place a high value on 'self-directed learning', on 'negotiated curricula', and on 'cafeteria-style' curricula. They may all be seen as ways in which a monolithic educational system is progressively being transformed to accommodate the right of learners to choose what to study and to enable them to exploit public educational resources for their own purposes.

Can thesis 1 be reconciled with a national core curriculum or is it so hopelessly incompatible with it that, if thesis 1 is valid, the case for a national core curriculum would be weakened?

While the educational scenario depicted by thesis 1 has several attractive features, it is necessary to establish that these are not ruled out by the introduction of a national core curriculum. It is sometimes maintained, for example, that a curriculum based on pupil choice offers limitless opportunities for enterprising teaching/learning strategies, whereas a national core curriculum is likely to be educationally stultifying and to entail 'traditional' or 'formal' teaching. Of course, the introduction of a core curriculum entails no such thing. Even if such a framework took the form of a mere list of compulsory subjects for all pupils, the nature of the teaching/learning strategies to be used would still have to be determined.

Clearly, school subjects offer unlimited scope for enquiry, for pupils to find out for themselves, for investigation, for hypothesis testing, for the evaluation of evidence, for effective communication and much else besides. Indeed, teachers who failed to incorporate such approaches into their work could not be said to be teaching a subject at all. The enterprising pedagogy that is implied by thesis 1 may feature just as prominently in a national core curriculum. Indeed, it is conceivable that a national curricular framework might include guidelines which required schools to ensure that whatever subjects were compulsory had to be treated in ways that recognised that each subject, properly taught, was a powerful resource for the development of all kinds of thinking and other skills.

In the same way, it is often assumed that the introduction of a core curriculum requires that areas of knowledge must be regarded as absolute and must be assimilated by pupils in a totally uncritical and unquestioning way, in marked contrast to the approach to knowledge implied by thesis 1. Again, the introduction of a core curriculum carries no such implication. It is a caricature of subjects to present them merely as slabs of knowledge that simply have to be transmitted to pupils. Indeed, each area of knowledge is a source of considerable controversy and debate amongst practitioners; and to 'do' a subject properly is to participate in these very debates and to come to realise the provisional status of knowledge.

Clarification of these potential misunderstandings should suggest that there are many ways in which thesis 1 is perfectly compatible with a core curriculum. Indeed, as was maintained above, a national core curriculum might require that those features of thesis 1 to which attention has been drawn should be the essential features of the curriculum of all pupils. However, the essential feature of thesis 1 concerns the principle of pupil choice. To what extent is that principle compatible with the notion that there are certain areas of learning that should be essential for all pupils? Thesis 1 would certainly be incompatible with a core curriculum which consisted of a comprehensive and detailed specification covering every aspect of every subject. However, no-one seriously advocates the kind of national curriculum in which a uniform diet is rigidly and unsparingly dispensed to all. If that conception of a core curriculum is set aside there are at least three ways in which pupil choice can be accommodated within a core curriculum.

First, a core curriculum may take the form of a number of divisions of study each consisting of a range of cognate activities, with the requirement that pupils should select at least one subject or activity from each division. For example, the curricular offerings of a school may be structured under a number of headings as follows:

Communication	Mathematical Studies	Social Studies	Sciences	Aesthetic Studies
English	Mathematics	History	Physics	Art
French	Arithmetic	Geography	Chemistry	Music
Latin	Statistics	Economics	Biology	Craft
German	etc.	Sociology	Gen. Science	Physical Educ.
etc.		Modern Studies	Engineering	Drama
		Politics	etc.	etc.
		etc.		

Pupils may derive their programme by choosing at least one subject from each of these 'option columns'. This mode of curriculum organisation is extremely common in Britain. In North America, where credit and modular systems of curriculum organisation are the norm, even more provision can be made for pupil choice because the number of curricular offerings in each column can be very extensive indeed. For example, in the typical American high school, there may be as many as twenty offerings under 'Communication', including such programmes as 'The American Novel', 'The Negro in Literature', 'Society and Literature', 'Creative Writing', 'Shakespeare', and so on. While the scope for choice is very considerably increased in this way, usually pupils are required to select three or four units of work from such divisions of study. Clearly, then, it is possible, by organising the curriculum in this way, to ensure that 'essential' areas of study are covered while, at the same time, acknowledging the importance of pupil choice. Nearer home, the national initiative for the education of 16–18 year-olds in Scotland – known as Action Plan – has incorporated this approach and, to date, more than 2,000 units of work have been prepared and form part of a nationwide structure of provision which is intended to accommodate student choice and self-pacing. Indeed, the same 'modularisation' of provision may be extended to the Higher Grade, the traditional school-leaving examination for 17–18 year-olds in Scotland.

An alternative way of effecting this kind of reconciliation of choice and compulsion is through the familiar 'core plus options' form of curriculum organisation. In this approach, certain curricular requirements are laid down and made compulsory for all pupils – the 'core' of the curriculum – while the remainder of pupils' total programme of study consists of options which are drawn from as many alternatives as the school can make available. Sometimes, as in the Munn proposals in Scotland to be considered later, provision is also made for pupils to exercise choice within the core as well as within the optional area of the curriculum.

The third way of accommodating pupil choice within a core curriculum is perhaps even more important than the two approaches to curriculum structure that have just been considered. Current arrangements are frequently criticised on the grounds that the only concession they make to the principle of pupil choice is to allow pupils to choose which subjects to study and that choice is exercised perhaps twice throughout a full secondary school experience. Thesis 1, however, goes far beyond this 'organisational' choice and argues for pupil choice at the classroom level. Choice at that level implies that opportunities exist for pupils to chart their own way through a programme of study – to concentrate on certain objectives rather than others, to select those assignments that most closely relate to their own interests, to move at a pace dictated by their own needs rather than those of the class group, to opt for modes of assessment which they find least uncongenial, and so on. This kind of curriculum negotiation is an important feature of thesis 1. Since it is an approach which recognises the developing maturity of learners, and seeks to enlist their full participation in the development of their skills and understanding, there are grounds for insisting that it ought to characterise all teaching and learning in the middle and later years of the secondary school. There is no reason why a national core curriculum framework should rule out such approaches: indeed, such a framework might very well stipulate that the teaching/learning strategies to be adopted in each of the required areas of study should have these very characteristics.

So far, the analysis has suggested that there is no serious incompatibility between thesis 1 and the idea of a national core curriculum. It has been shown that many of the desiderata entailed by thesis 1 are equally realisable through a core of compulsory studies. In addition, it has been argued that such a core curriculum can accommodate the exercise of pupil choice at both the organisational and classroom levels. However, the radical version of thesis 1 insists on complete freedom of choice for pupils to pursue only those activities that interest them. There would appear to be no possibility of reconciliation here: on the one hand it is maintained that there are certain activities that should feature in the curriculum of all pupils; on the other it is contended that there should be no prescription and that the curriculum should reflect only those activities which pupils themselves are disposed to pursue. How is this fundamental challenge to the core curriculum to be met? It is to be met surely by questioning whether the radical version of thesis 1 is really sustainable. There are four arguments which may be invoked to demonstrate that it is not.

The first argument concerns the social functions of education and insists that, if young people are to be enabled to participate effectively in the various roles of adult life, they require to engage in activities that prepare them for these roles. That is to say, there are certain activities that have such a crucial contribution to make to the development of young people and their capacity to cope with life in a complex society that we are justified in making them compulsory elements in the school curriculum, whether or not pupils find them interesting. The second argument maintains that if, as the proponents of the radical version of thesis 1 urge, autonomy and self-determination are the central ideas of responsible living, it must be recognised that these cannot be exercised properly without a great deal of prior educational effort. Responsible choice of activities to pursue, or lifestyles to adopt, implies familiarity with a range of alternatives; in addition, it presupposes a capacity for discriminating, for evaluating evidence, for adopting a critical approach to the circumstances of living, and for making reasonably sophisticated appraisals of the human condition. But all of these require the kind of careful attention and nurturing that a school curriculum seeks to provide. Thirdly, to restrict pupils' education to activities which they find interesting is to offer an unacceptably restricted educational experience to pupils. It is to fail to recognise that, while pupils cannot be compelled to be interested in anything, their interests can nevertheless be activated by good teaching. Indeed, it is perhaps the *raison d'etre* of the teacher to engender and cultivate interests and to extend the range of interests that young people might come to develop. Finally, the *laissez-faire* approach that is implied by the radical version of thesis 1 fails to acknowledge that if pupils are simply left to their own devices to develop whatever interests they happen to encounter they may become the victims of an environment which may be dangerously impoverished if not totally anti-educational. If pupils are left to fend for themselves in this way, what assurance have we, or they, that they will encounter the sorts of experience that, it has been argued above, engender the kind of autonomy that is so highly cherished?

These arguments constitute powerful grounds for rejecting the radical version of thesis 1. There is an overwhelming case for placing pupils in contexts in which they will acquire the skills and understandings necessary for responsible living. If autonomy is essential to that form of life then it should be made an explicit curricular objective and seen as the outcome of a rationally planned series of learning experiences. There need be no fear that pupils are being enslaved to other people's ideas and values since the function of curricular activities is to develop pupils' capacity for critical rationality and independent-mindedness; it is to equip them with 'the tools of autonomy'. It is concluded, therefore, that the idea of a core curriculum has survived its first test. It can fully accommodate requirements that learners should be self-directed, that there should be provision for curriculum negotiation, and that the curriculum should cultivate autonomy. Moreover, it can provide opportunities for pupil choice both with regard to areas of study and modes of learning. However, the core curriculum cannot be reconciled with the claim that pupils should have complete freedom to choose, but that version of the pupil choice thesis is scarcely sustainable in the light of the above analysis.

Thesis 2: Differentiation

Thesis 2 concerns the extent to which the curriculum should seek to cultivate individual differences and take account of intellectual and other differences between pupils. There are two versions of the thesis.

The first version has it that a society consists of unique individuals and that a healthy society is one in which human individuality is fostered. One of the ways of recognising that principle is through the cultivation of individual differences in schools and through enabling pupils to develop their talents to the highest level so that they can make a special and distinctive contribution to social life. In this way, the richness and diversity of social life is protected and perpetuated. The introduction of a core curriculum may threaten that richness and diversity and substitute a drab uniformity in which individuality is eclipsed.

Leaving aside the issue of whether the cultivation of individual differences is more important than the fostering of characteristics which people share in common – and it is not self-evidently true that it is – two points can be made in reply. In the first place, a national core curriculum would not eliminate all scope for pupils to develop their distinctive talents. Both of the modes of curriculum organisation considered on page 45 will give pupils adequate opportunity to cultivate what they consider to be their particular strengths to as high a level as they wish. These highly developed capacities may thereafter provide a pathway into employment or act as a means of contributing in other ways to the life of a community.

In the second place, a core curriculum that is concerned to equip pupils with the capacity for autonomous decision-making will free pupils to adopt the kind of lifestyle they find congenial. In such circumstances, there is no reason why there should be any diminution in social diversity. Indeed, a core curriculum that actually encouraged pupils to explore occupational, domestic and sex roles critically instead of accepting these as sanctified by tradition would, if anything, enhance the richness and diversity of social life. In no sense, therefore, can a core curriculum be seen as a means of eliminating individual differences and of imposing uniformity of taste and lifestyle.

The more familiar version of thesis 2 concerns the differences in ability that are to be found in pupils. Its proponents point to the tremendous variation in human performance. However that variation is to be explained, it cannot, in the judgement of very many, be explained away. To put it in as neutral a way as possible, pupils differ in the rate at which they learn. How, then, are all pupils to cope with the demands of a core curriculum? If all pupils are to be expected to reach the same level of achievement across the range of compulsory activities, will it not be necessary to pitch the required standard at a ludicrously low level in order to accommodate those who experience most difficulty with school activities? In that event, what becomes of the brightest pupils? Are they to be held back and required to move at a pace determined by slower learners? On the other hand, if the required standard of achievement is pitched at a level that will challenge the brightest pupils, what is to become of those whose progress in school work is painstakingly slow, not to mention those with special educational needs? Whatever the standard of achievement expected, is it proposed that, irrespective of ability, all pupils should be expected to cover the same curricular ground? Does the core curriculum require the adoption of mixed-ability grouping, with all the pedagogical and organisational difficulties that entails?

That line of questioning is pursued by those who see the introduction of a core curriculum as educationally retrogressive. They point to the way in which, over the years, teachers have struggled to adapt the curriculum to the child rather than vice versa and have sought to devise programmes of work suited to the age, aptitude and ability of pupils. These developments led not to the introduction of a common programme of compulsory studies but to highly differentiated programmes and to forms of individualised learning which sought to engage pupils in work that was suited to the rate at which they learned and the mode of learning which they found congenial. These developments towards highly differentiated programmes were judged to be absolutely necessary in the light of pupil differences and in recognition of the fact that the conventional grammar school curriculum, with its heavily academic orientation, was an inappropriate and frequently unpalatable diet for very many pupils. Why, then, should the trend towards differentiation of curricula be apparently reversed by the introduction of a core of compulsory studies for all?

The case for differentiation in the curriculum to take account of differences in pupils' rates of learning is undoubtedly a strong one. It is true that conventional modes of differentiation – the division of pupils into separate types of school at the stage of transfer to secondary education and their allocation to radically different programmes – have been discredited. While the arguments which led to an abandonment of this traditional arrangement focused mainly on the inequalities of selection and the social and the educational effects of separating children into different schools, at least part of the case rested on a dissatisfaction at the curricular consequences of a selective system. That system posited radically different educational objectives and programmes of study for pupils in the different types of secondary school. Broadly, three programmes were made available, corresponding to three types of secondary school: one that consisted of study in the conventional academic subjects and was preoccupied with pupils' intellectual development; one that was oriented strongly towards technical and technological studies; and one that engaged pupils largely in practical activities and that was broadly related to a range of relatively low-level occupations. However well-intentioned, this curricular arrangement had the effect of seriously distorting the education of young people and depriving them, in different ways, of a properly balanced programme. The introduction of comprehensive secondary education did not put an end to attempts at curricular differentiation: two curricular traditions were continued within the walls of the comprehensive school – the programme of academic activities for the ablest and a more practically oriented programme for those who were judged to be unsuited to the academic course. That curricular dualism was strongly defended. For example, Bantock[1] defended the practice of differentiating the curriculum and favoured the development of a distinctive programme for pupils 'who show little aptitude for the cognitively based curriculum'. Such a curriculum, in Bantock's judgement, should involve the arts, 'practical common life', television and photography and other media, and physical activities. While Bantock made it clear that his proposal should not be regarded as an 'inferior sop handed out to the inadequate' that, indeed, is how proposals of the kind advocated by him have tended to be regarded. How, then, can the curriculum be differentiated, given that the same broad curricular objectives exist for all pupils? There are two possible approaches.

The first has been adopted in the development programme in Scotland following the Munn and Dunning reports of 1977. With the introduction of a national curriculum framework and a national assessment and certification system embracing all pupils, a way had to be found of recognising different levels of achievement. The strategy adopted was to posit three levels of award at 16+ – Foundation level, General level, and Credit level – and to specify as clearly as possible the skills and understandings that would be tested at each level. In addition, differentiated programmes of study were in some cases devised to correspond to the three award levels. The justification for this approach is that in each of the recognised areas of the curriculum pupils should undertake a programme that is appropriate in the sense that it offers a challenging educational experience but one in which success is possible without being guaranteed. In some areas, for example in English, there is a common syllabus structure and the differentiation is reflected in the levels of achievement pupils attain in the course work and in the end of course examination. In other areas, for example in Mathematics, there are separate syllabuses corresponding to the three award levels. The different syllabuses have been carefully structured to achieve a degree of overlap and to facilitate transfer from one level to another depending on a pupil's progress. Thus, while the General programme is more demanding than the Foundation programme, it will nevertheless presuppose that the skills and understandings demanded at Foundation level have, indeed, been achieved and will engage pupils in more demanding activities. In the same way, the Credit syllabus will assume that the competences demanded at the General level have been achieved and will engage pupils in the most demanding of the three syllabus levels. At the same time, there is no direct relationship between a syllabus and the level of award that is obtained: that is, the level of award is not narrowly predetermined.

A second approach finds its most succinct expression in Bruner's dictum: 'Any subject can be taught effectively in some intellectually honest form to any child at any stage of development.'[2] That provocative assertion encapsulates one of the central principles of what has come to be called 'mastery learning'. In this view, differences in school performance are not to be explained by invoking latent characteristics such as 'ability'. On the contrary, variations in achievement can be explained by reference to what learners know and can do prior to the start of a course, their own commitment to learning and to achievement, and the quality of the instruction they receive. Accordingly, pupils' achievements are likely to be improved if steps are taken to ensure that units of work are clearly related to, and build on, their previous achievements; if pupils can be encouraged to adopt a positive attitude to their work and to believe that success is possible for them; and if the teaching strategies involve the clear articulation of the competences sought

curriculum represents a selection of knowledge that is bound to be arbitrary.

The same arbitrariness is detected in the division of knowledge and in the manner of its pursuit. The 'compartmentalisation' of knowledge into different subjects is taken to represent the demarcation lines devised by scholars to preserve their territory and to protect their vested interests. At the same time, notions such as rationality, respect for evidence, logical argument, the values that are traditionally thought to underpin any serious intellectual pursuit, are also taken to be suspect for these values are themselves considered to be socially constructed: they reflect merely how certain influential groups of scholars perceive their work and cannot claim to be the inescapable and essential conditions for the pursuit of scholarly activity.

This account of the relativity of knowledge tends to be accompanied by an account of the acquisition of knowledge as a thoroughly subjective undertaking. Since knowledge is taken to have no independent and objective existence outside the knower, knowledge acquisition is envisaged not as the passive absorption of the constructs that have been used and accumulated by others, or as the progressive and systematic initiation into structured areas of disciplined activity, but as an individualistic process of imposing meaning through self-activated interaction with the world. Thus, for example, one advocate of open education has insisted that 'every child is a self-activated maker of meaning, an active agent in his own learning process . . . a self-reliant, independent, self-actualising individual'; besides, there is no 'inherently indispensable body of knowledge that every child should know . . . what two children carry in their heads as "chair" or "aunt" or "black" will never be absolutely identical'.[3]

In writings of this kind, the relativity of knowledge and the subjectivity of knowledge acquisition reinforce each other: indeed, in a world in which knowledge and its pursuit are merely arbitrary forms of conventional behaviour, the learners' perception of what is valuable must be as valid as any other. Manifestly, thesis 3 is hopelessly irreconcilable with the case for a core of compulsory studies. If one curriculum is no better than any other the core curriculum is bound to be interpreted as merely an arbitrary imposition. There could scarcely be a more direct challenge to the idea of a framework of educationally valuable activities into which all children are to be initiated. Mary Warnock is one of those who has been clear about the dangers of thesis 3.

> If creeping relativism is not rooted out then it seems to me that educationalists might as well shut up shop. Not only in theory but in practice as well, relativism tends to sap the confidence of curriculum makers and teachers; and rightly. For confidence in their own curriculum would be nothing but a sign of dogmatism, according to the theory.[4]

Can the challenge of 'creeping relativism' be met?

There are several counters to the position expressed in thesis 3. First, if that thesis is correct in its relativist stance that we are faced with various different perspectives on truth and reality, each of equal validity with none having an overriding claim on our allegiance, and if there really is no way of demonstrating conclusively that one view is superior to another, why should that thesis itself be taken seriously? Since the thesis rejects the possibility of objective truth the relativist thesis itself cannot aspire to that status and is therefore unworthy of serious attention. Relativism, in other words, is a self-contradictory and logically incoherent position: its adherents may be imagined somewhere up the tree of knowledge resolutely sawing off the branch that is supporting them!

The second counter argument relates to the claim that fields of knowledge and modes of disciplined enquiry are arbitrary. That criticism derives from the view that what counts as knowledge and the means of advancing knowledge merely reflect the preferences of particularly powerful groups of scholars and could therefore make no claim to objectivity. It must be obvious that the various traditions of intellectual and other forms of enquiry are indeed man-made, in the sense that they have been developed by individuals and have grown out of social life. To concede that, however, is not to concede that these fields of knowledge must therefore be arbitrary. On the contrary, these traditions of enquiry and reflection are rule-governed: they have built into them procedures and analytical techniques for distinguishing between what is true and what is false. What is more, their proper conduct requires a commitment to rationality, to respect for evidence, to impartiality and to truth. The view that these values themselves are merely social conventions fails to acknowledge that without agreement on, and commitment to, these values, intellectual and other forms of disciplined activity simply cannot be conducted. Indeed, those who advocate thesis 3 are bound to have a commitment to such values if they are to present a case that makes any kind of sense, for these are the values which underpin any thesis that is to be taken seriously. It cannot be emphasised too strongly that the basic questions concerning what counts as knowledge and truth and rationality are not to be settled by invoking the views of any particular group such as teachers or academics. These issues are not settled by an appeal to authority of that kind: they are settled by the analysis of appropriate evidence. It is precisely these publicly agreed analytical procedures which constitute the source of the objectivity of knowledge.

Thirdly, the fact that, over the years, changes of perspective, even of a fundamental character, are encountered cannot be taken as evidence of the relativity of knowledge. As has been argued, there are public procedures for determining whether or not knowledge has been established. At any given time, activity within any of these fields of knowledge will involve the testing of new hypotheses and the search for more sophisticated explanations of the social, the human and the physical conditions. In that sense, all knowledge is provisional. But the fact that today's established truths can be overturned by fresh inquiry does not demonstrate that all explanations are equally possible and valuable and that none is to be preferred to any other. It is manifestly the case that not all explanations and theories are possible: only those explanations are objective which meet certain public and objective criteria. The fact that these criteria may change and evolve over the years does not in any sense weaken their objectivity.

Finally, the picture of knowledge acquisition implied by thesis 3 is open to serious criticism. The various fields of knowledge are not immutable slabs of content: they constitute areas of intellectual, artistic and other kinds of disciplined activity and inquiry. To engage in them is to develop the capacity to judge what is appropriate evidence for particular claims, rather than merely to accept uncritically what certain authorities declare to be the case. That conception of the process of acquiring knowledge is completely at odds with the idea that in learning an individual imposes his or her own meaning on the circumstances and experiences of life. That idiosyncratic view, which is entailed by thesis 3, fails to acknowledge that human development is not an individualistic enterprise: it is a matter of inheriting a tradition of shared meanings and public understandings. Children are in no position to impose their own categories on life and experience, for the basic categories which convey meaning are enshrined in the very language they are acquiring. If that were not the case children would be locked in a private world without the capacity to communicate with anyone. Of course, we may each maintain a rich world of subjective feelings and interpretations of personal experience, but that does not mean to say that in claiming to know something we can avoid the obligation to adduce appropriate evidence. Knowing, then, is not merely a matter of subjective judgement: it is to be capable of a form of human achievement which is governed by public criteria, and it is the existence of such public and agreed criteria that makes objective knowledge possible.

Thesis 3, it was acknowledged, constituted a significant threat to the notion of a national core curriculum. If knowledge simply reflected the preferences and values of dominant groups and lacked any kind of objective validity, what justification could there be for elevating certain fields of knowledge to the status of compulsory school activities for all? However, arguments have been advanced to demonstrate that this thesis is not sustainable and is, indeed, logically incoherent. But these arguments, even if they are valid, do not alter the fact that there are widely differing and conflicting philosophies of education and of life. In the face of such disagreements, how is a core curriculum to be identified? The institution of a national core curriculum implies a degree of consensus about aims and curriculum. Is such a consensus possible or, given the existence of deeply held and differing convictions, is a core curriculum an impossibility? There are several ways of responding to this line of criticism.

First, to hold that disagreements are so fundamental that any core selected is bound to be arbitrary is a recipe either for inertia or anarchy. From this point of view, *any* curriculum, whether it is devised by a national body, a local authority, or the teachers in a school, is bound to be the expression of what someone considers to be valuable and is also bound to be the source of disagreement; and any attempt to impose such a curriculum is bound to be interpreted as an indefensible display of arbitrary power. Should schools and their pupils, therefore, be left to do as they please, in the absence of agreed aims and curricula? But how is that policy to be defended? It surely is as arbitrary as any other. Clearly, therefore, to argue against a core curriculum on the grounds that agreement is unachievable is to end in a logical cul-de-sac.

Secondly, the existence of radical disagreement on educational issues does not imply that all views are equally tenable. Views are not valid simply because they are sincerely held. Besides, as was urged in the discussion of the relativity of knowledge, there are public and objective ways of discriminating between views and determining which are sustainable and which are not. It would be a mistake, therefore, to suppose that agreement on a core curriculum was an impossibility on the grounds that there were no means of objectively establishing whether a particular candidate for a core curriculum was, indeed, defensible. Clearly, there are.

Finally, conflicting philosophies about life and disagreements on fundamental values need not rule out the possibility of agreement on curricular aims. For one thing, widespread controversy may mask very extensive areas of agreement. For another, perhaps many of these disagreements are reconcilable. For example, there are those who insist that the curriculum should produce pupils who are equipped to meet the demands of the work-place, maintaining that the country's prosperity and economic productivity is paramount. Others, believing that we are moving into what has been called a post-industrial society, or, dismayed at rising unemployment, argue that pupils should be encouraged to acquire a range of skills and interests to pursue in their increased leisure time. Such differences are far from being irreconcilable. What is to prevent the advocates of such views from agreeing that a core curriculum should seek to achieve both desiderata and, at the same time, to equip pupils with the tools for discriminating between the lifestyles implied by the respective views? The thrust of this argument is that there may, indeed, be a good deal of common ground between the proponents of different educational and philosophical standpoints. Through patient discussion, analysis, consultation and negotiation it is conceivable that the area of agreement may be much broader than is sometimes supposed, broad enough to sustain a national core curriculum. Certainly, experience in other countries, even north of the border, where national core curricula have been introduced, suggests that consensus is possible and that pessimism and inertia may not be the most appropriate responses to the existence of disagreements.

Thesis 4: Cultural Pluralism

One of the recurring features of contemporary educational discussion is the demand for multicultural education, for arrangements and approaches which take cognisance of the fact that ours is a pluralistic society, one that is characterised by cultural diversity. The requirement that the curriculum should reflect and celebrate that cultural diversity and pluralism of values may, on the face of it, be incompatible with a core curriculum for all pupils. What, then, is meant by cultural pluralism and can a core curriculum accommodate what is implied by that term?

There are several features of cultural pluralism that are worth highlighting in the present context. First, it is usually taken to refer to the kind of society in which power is decentralised rather than concentrated excessively in central government agencies. It describes a society in which there is a proliferation of intermediate and special interest groups so that people have considerable scope for controlling their own affairs, for involvement in decision-making, for exerting pressure, and for influencing the shape of general social policy. This form of strongly participative democracy is seen as a way of preventing the excessive concentration of power, the rigid institution of two classes – the rulers and the ruled – and the emergence of political orthodoxes and forms of totalitarian control. Indeed, opportunities are created for people in their own cultural and other groupings to decide how their lives should be ordered, thus ensuring that they have a personal responsibility for policies and their effects.

Secondly, cultural pluralism implies a society which, far from being monolithically uniform, consists of a variety of different sub-cultures and groups with their own distinctive ethnic, religious, linguistic or cultural identity. It is widely accepted that, in the wake of massive migration and immigration of people for industrial and other reasons, most societies are characterised by diversity: they consist of many groups representing different national and cultural backgrounds. These minority groups, it is maintained, have a right to maintain their way of life and to make educational and other arrangements that enable their cultural traditions to be perpetuated. Of course, these ethnic, religious or linguistic sub-groups do not constitute the only significant minorities in the population. The 'host' culture itself is far from homogeneous: it consists of a whole range of sub-groups which derive from, for example, allegiance to a particular geographical locality, a particular sport or pastime, religious denomination, or a shared occupation. The extensive range of such sub-cultures that go to make up a society are the source of its richness and of the vitality of social life. Their protection is considered essential as a means of preserving the quality of life against the deadening effects of mass culture and consumerism. Indeed, the co-existence of such diverse groups and the sharing of traditions which that entails can be mutually enriching and serve to create an enhanced and revitalised common culture.

Thirdly, the social diversity that is created by the existence of a variety of identifiable sub-groups and sub-cultures is reinforced by the existence of a multiplicity of lifestyles. These have been generated by the exposure to patterns of life and behaviour elsewhere that results from foreign travel; by population mobility; by the prevailing lack of consensus on the characteristics of the good life; and by the astonishing variety of behaviour and attitudes that are communicated through the mass media. Furthermore, there has been a progressive erosion of gender specific norms of behaviour, with the result that social expectations with regard to male and female roles are much less rigidly restrictive, where they have not disappeared entirely. The combined effect of such developments is that individuals are now faced with an almost unlimited variety of models of behaviour and lifestyles.

Finally, cultural pluralism involves a commitment to values which guarantee the perpetuation of diversity – the right to freedom of association, freedom of speech, freedom of choice and tolerance. These values, when combined with the other characteristics of cultural pluralism mentioned, create the conditions in which social diversity flourishes. Individuals, freed from the restricting influence of tradition, of churches, of schools, even of family life, can select from a welter of lifestyles, and social groups have the knowledge that, however eccentric a tradition they represent, their eccentricity will be tolerated and protected.

On the face of it, cultural pluralism would appear to rule out a national core curriculum. The institution of such a core would appear to conflict with the notion that power should be decentralised and that schools themselves ought to be allowed to work out their own educational salvation. A core curriculum might, indeed, be regarded as a form of cultural imperialism, and as an affront to the 'democracy of belief'. The advocates of the thesis might argue further that to institutionalise a core of essential learnings for all is to invoke the 'melting-pot' theory of education, the process through which successive waves of immigrants to the USA were 'Americanised' by a common schooling. Such an approach, far from celebrating human and cultural diversity in ways that the proponents of multicultural education urge, appears instead to be designed to ensure that such differences are obliterated. Are the claims on behalf of cultural pluralism on the one hand and a core curriculum on the other quite so emphatically irreconcilable?

To answer that question it is necessary first to examine in more detail the values inherent in cultural pluralism. Such an analysis has been undertaken by Crittenden.[5] One of the most significant features of that analysis is the conclusion that cultural pluralism does not involve the institution, within a host culture, of a variety of distinctive ethnic groups which are concerned to maintain and preserve the way of life of the country of origin at all times, to preserve their separateness from the host culture, and resolutely to assert their exclusiveness. That is, cultural pluralism presupposes that minority groups, ethnic or otherwise, are part of a coherent society, sharing in its way of life and not merely constituting a collection of cultural ghettos. That implies the sharing of a common language, the acceptance of a common legal framework, and rational acquiescence in a common political order and in the basic social morality without which a society could not exist. These, arguably, are requirements for the maintenance of any kind of social life. A pluralist society requires, in addition, a commitment to further values – autonomy, tolerance, rationality, respect for persons, non-violent means of persuasion, fairness, freedom of speech and so on. Of these, Crittenden places particular emphasis on rationality. He postulates a society in which there are public criteria for discriminating between values and styles of life; in which there is a commitment to the critical scrutiny of existing social practices in the interests of enabling rationally defensible alternative lifestyles and views to flourish. Indeed, without such a commitment to critical rationality, Crittenden maintains, pluralism could not survive. If, then, cultural pluralism rests on certain values and understandings that have to be acquired if a pluralist society is to be maintained, there is a case for establishing a core of common learnings that prepare pupils for life in such a society. The core of essential learnings identified by Crittenden turns out to be extensive and includes the following:

(a) 'the development of an adequate understanding of the principles of the basic social morality and the views on which pluralism depends';

(b) 'an introduction to at least the main features of the political, legal and economic system within which the members of the society live.' The study of the economic system is taken to include the pattern of government and private control, the way in which income and other goods are distributed, the lines of access to various forms of employment, the trade unions, etc.

(c) 'the acquisition of skills of speaking, reading and writing English as the common language. The purpose is not simply to develop these skills as a code for basic communication but also as a medium for the expressive and celebratory aspects of the life in which everyone participates as a member of the same society and a sharer in its evolving distinctive culture.'

(d) the development of rationality and the particular skills and knowledge required for the rational discussion of controversial social issues and for detecting the various forms of non-rational political and commercial persuasion . . . including 'the skills and attitudes required for the rational analysis and discussion of issues on which members of a pluralist society may seriously differ'.

Crittenden makes it clear that such a core curriculum would constitute the very minimum requirements for preparing pupils for life in a culturally pluralist society. In the event, therefore, thesis 4, far from demonstrating the indefensibility of a core curriculum, actually depends for *its* validity on the existence of just such a core curriculum.

Thesis 5: Decentralisation of Power

Opponents of a national core curriculum frequently base their case on the claim that curricular decisions should be made locally and not nationally. The existing statutory position is invoked in defence of this contention. It is maintained that, while the Secretary of State has the general responsibility 'to promote the education of the people' and 'to secure the effective execution by local authorities, under his control and direction, of the national policy for providing for a varied and comprehensive educational service in every area', existing legislation nevertheless protects the rights of local education authorities in curriculum matters: it insists that 'the secular instruction to be given to pupils shall . . . be under the control of the local education authority', and that the local education authority should 'determine the general character of the school and its place in the local educational system'. Furthermore, governors of schools 'have the general direction of the conduct and the curriculum of the school'. Of course, the existing legal position is not in any sense logically binding: it is modifiable if, in the light of experience, it proved unworkable or unsatisfactory in other ways. Are there grounds, then, for defending the existing statutory position, which clearly leaves curriculum control in the hands of local education authorities?

Defenders of that position, in line with the advocates of cultural pluralism, maintain that in a healthy democracy there should be considerable decentralisation of decision-making. They claim the right of local and other groups to make decisions on matters that deeply affect their lives. They maintain, moreover, that educational arrangements are best made locally, by people with an intimate knowledge of local conditions, of employment opportunities, of distinctive geographical and other characteristics of an area, of the needs of industry and commerce, as well as the needs of families and their children. Among the local groups that are thought to have an important role to play both at local authority and school level are parents. Their entitlement to a say in the education of their children is enshrined in legislation and the Taylor Report[6] on the management of schools strongly supported parental and 'lay' involvement in curriculum decision-making and control. The basic argument for local control is that a curriculum designed by local people will reflect the needs of local, neighbourhood and community life in a way that a national programme put together by anonymous bureaucrats in Whitehall, or wherever, could not match. Such a curriculum, it is felt, is more responsive: it can be adapted easily and quickly to accommodate rapid and unexpected changes in local conditions, just as small ships can change direction more easily and swiftly than large tankers. Furthermore, local education authorities run, manage and resource the schools and, in consequence, are bound to have responsibility for the kind of education schools provide. How can a particular curriculum be implemented if insufficient resources are made available to sustain it? Bill Gatherer, the Chief Advisor in Lothian Region, defends this position in these terms:

> One might, certainly, pursue the argument that in a democratic state educational policies should be formed at the sources of authority and that the education authority *is* a major source of authority. But that leads one into controversies about the nature of authority and legitimation.
>
> I do, however, argue that policies should be formed at the sources of *economic* provision, so that we can regulate our aspirations to match our practical capabilities. This is not an aridly materialistic assertion: at any stage in the process towards the ideal state of affairs it is necessary to know how far it is realistic to go and how best your available resources can be utilised. This is a pragmatic argument for more effective policy-making at local level and I maintain that educational policy formation must include curriculum policy formation.[7]

Thesis 5 insists that it is at the local level that curriculum control should be exercised for it is at that level that curricular needs can be identified and the necessary resources and support made available to ensure that these needs are met in relation to an integrated and comprehensive range of public services. The question is sometimes put directly: How can the Secretary of State exercise comparable curricular control when he lacks the detailed information that effective curriculum planning requires, and when he does not run the schools, appoint the teachers, or make available the resources?

The final justification for thesis 5 is related to the deep-seated fear that central control of the curriculum would lead to political indoctrination, to the purveying of 'state-approved knowledge', and the moulding of pupils in accordance with the official specification. Central control of the curriculum is held to presage the end of liberty and the onset of totalitarianism. This fear has been expressed by Geoffrey Caston, a former Joint Secretary of the Schools Council, in a defence of pluralism or 'the dispersal of power in education'. He writes:

> Education is an area of social activity in which the concentration of power can severely damage young people. They are, after all, compulsory inmates of the schools, and thus, in a very real sense, their prisoners. This is so even though the purpose of their imprisonment by society is not punitive but beneficient. It nevertheless involves the exercise of power over them; it is forceful intervention in their personal development. They can be harmed by the misuse of this power so as to mould them in the image of the state. Or, to put it in a less sinister way, by treating them as instruments of some national manpower policy rather than as self-determining individuals.[8]

While these and other arguments are adduced in defence of local control and the maintenance of local democracy in curriculum matters, the available evidence suggests that that control is not exercised too assiduously. The evidence submitted to the Taylor Committee and the responses by local authorities to the government's circular 14.77, demonstrate clearly enough that local education authorities are content to leave curricular decisions to schools. And Gatherer, in the article quoted above, observes rather gloomily of the Scottish scene: 'Local authorities in Scotland have no genuine status in the management of the curriculum and so they are left dangling between the unitary power of the Scottish Education Department on the one hand and the chaotic power of isolated headteachers on the other.' However, evidence of this kind does not weaken the central thrust of thesis 5: curriculum control *should* not be concentrated at the centre. Can a national core curriculum accommodate demands for the decentralisation of curriculum decision-making?

It has to be acknowledged in the first place that the rights of local authorities on curriculum matters can never be regarded as absolute: their rights must always be circumscribed by considerations relating to the national interest. It would be against the national interest, for example, if as a matter of deliberate policy an LEA's curricular provision was so structured that it severely affected pupils' opportunities for access to higher education, or led to marked discrepancies in curricular provision between one LEA and another, or if blatantly racist or sexist curriculum policies were officially sanctioned by an LEA. If that argument is accepted, if, that is, it is agreed that the claims of local democracy are not absolute but are subject always to an overriding national interest, whoever has responsibility for protecting that, then the way is clear for a reconciliation between thesis 5 and a national core curriculum. There are several ways in which such a reconciliation might be effected.

First, it could be granted that all of the arguments adduced in support of local democracy and local control were valid. Of course, local authorities are well placed to determine local needs, to be responsive to local requirements and, in effect, to control curricular provision through control of resources. All of these powers could be protected if all that was proposed was a curriculum framework which ensured that every pupil received an adequate education in areas of learning that were considered to be essential. The actual details in each of the required areas would need to be worked out, and responsibility for that would clearly lie with local authorities and their staff. Obviously, an LEA would fill out the curricular details in ways which suited local conditions and which took account of what could be resourced.

The second way of reconciling the claims of local democracy with a national core curriculum would also concede most of the points made in thesis 5. It might then be postulated that what was being determined nationally was not a total curriculum, but only the central core of a curriculum. The national requirement might amount to as much as half of a pupil's total programme and the remainder would be determined at the LEA or school level. Presumably, in these circumstances, an LEA would exploit the optional area of the curriculum as it saw fit: it would seek to ensure that it fully reflected local conditions and was in the interests of its pupils.

The third approach to reconciliation is even more generous for it would combine the features of the first two. It might be maintained that what was nationally required was not a complete curriculum and not even a clearly defined and specified core; rather, to what LEAs would be expected to acquiesce would be the framework of a core, an outline of the key areas that would feature in the curriculum of every pupil. It would be for LEAs themselves to provide the detailed working out of what it preferred to see in each of the core areas. An arrangement of this kind is a far cry from the prescribing of state-approved knowledge and the stuffing of pupils' heads with political orthodoxes.

Finally, the anxieties revealed in thesis 5 might be allayed by ensuring that nothing was finally decided upon nationally, not even in broad outline, until there had been full consultation with the LEAs and their staff to ensure that the national core framework reflected as full a consensus as possible. A core curriculum devised in this way would surely meet the central objections incorporated in thesis 5. It represents, in effect, the kind of partnership between national government and local education authority which the current legislation articulates, albeit somewhat ambiguously, and to which successive Secretaries of State, north and south of the border, are apparently committed. Their initiatives can be interpreted as attempts to ensure that both national and local agencies accept the responsibilities which partnership in curriculum control implies.

Thesis 6: Professional Autonomy of Teachers

Thesis 6 has features in common with thesis 5: it is strongly critical of moves to locate curriculum control at the centre and echoes the demand, in the prevailing climate of participation, for local involvement in curriculum decision-making. In thesis 6, however, the involvement that is considered imperative is that of teachers. Teachers, as the professionals, are considered to know best. The curriculum is considered to be their *métier*. They have the experience of working with pupils and planning learning activities that take full account of pupils' varying educational needs; they are by training and qualification the one professional group that is competent to decide on curriculum matters; and since, moreover, they have to implement whatever curriculum policy emerges, the responsibility for determining that curriculum should rest with them.

Curriculum decisions are therefore best taken, not by politicians, but by teachers acting autonomously. That view of the professional autonomy of teachers has been defended in these terms, again by Geoffrey Caston:

> For educators, the essence of professionalism lies in the exercise by individuals of choice and judgement in the interests, not of ourselves or our employers, but of our clients: in this case our pupils. These choices must be made in terms of a professional ethic which includes an obligation by the educator to provide service in an impartial way to all pupils, regardless of any private preferences between them that he may have. The obligation to the trouble-maker, the drug taker, is equal to the obligation to the academic or athletic star. Professionalism also includes an obligation to provide this service in the light of all the relevant and up-to-date information which the practitioner can muster. Educators must also be learners, from our own colleagues, from other professions, not least perhaps from our own pupils. Within this double ethic – of impartiality and open-mindedness – the professional can deny any outside authority the right to tell him how to do his job.[9]

Not surprisingly, teachers have looked upon the growing interest of central government in curriculum matters with deep suspicion and hostility. One teachers union official has described these developments as 'totalitarian'; another has attacked such 'interference' as further evidence of the way in which the work of teachers is 'plagued with more amateur experts, more ignorant know-alls, more pompously pontificating pundits, and more arrogant bureaucrats'.[10]

Several recent educational developments have helped to strengthen the professional autonomy of teachers in ways which would appear to weaken the case for a centrally determined core curriculum. One of the most significant of these is the shift in the style of curriculum development. In the early 1960s, when the school curriculum first began to attract systematic and critical attention, the most commonly adopted strategy was one in which groups of experts in particular areas of the curriculum developed new materials, piloted them in schools, modified them in the light of trials, then disseminated them as extensively as possible. It was a matter for professional pride on the part of such developers that the materials devised were 'teacher-proof' in the sense that all reasonable precautions had been taken to minimise the chances that the materials could be mishandled by teachers. That approach to curriculum development, which involved the central preparation of materials and their subsequent dissemination to all parts – hence the term 'the centre-periphery model' – did not always have the impact on teachers' professional practice that was expected of it, although in the educationally compact entity of Scotland it has been used with remarkable effectiveness. Several explanations have been offered for this state of affairs: it has been claimed, for example, that such a 'top-down' model made teachers feel that they were being coerced; that the materials, having been prepared in a remote centre, failed to take account of local conditions; and that teachers were denied the resources and support necessary for effective implementation of the materials in the classroom. Current approaches to curriculum development, having acknowledged the weaknesses in the centre-periphery model, seek to locate the origins of curriculum revitalisation not in a development agency but in individual schools; they seek to strengthen teachers' willingness and capacity to assume responsibility for the development of their own curricula.

School-based curriculum development implies that the curriculum of a school, the totality of the learning experiences it provides, should be a focus of continuing scrutiny by all staff concerned. It is now acknowledged that the only way of maintaining and enhancing the quality of the curriculum is to ensure that teachers have the necessary expertise and support to monitor and evaluate what they are doing and the commitment and resourcefulness to act in ways suggested by that evaluation. This kind of systematic self-study is now recognised to be an essential feature of teachers' professional activity: it is the means whereby they progressively sharpen their understanding of their own professional circumstances, and, in so doing, better their teaching. Moreover, by strengthening and supporting teachers' self-evaluation, schools can ensure that the curriculum is continuously monitored and modified to take account of changing requirements.

To conceive of teaching in this way, to see it as a form of research activity in which new approaches are tested and monitored, and in which classroom judgements are continuously informed by the best available evidence, is to recognise that it is a highly complex and demanding professional activity. The teacher as researcher or as 'extended' professional, with a continuing commitment to innovation, is manifestly far removed from the idea of the teacher as low-level functionary, dutifully and routinely dancing to someone else's tune. How, it is asked, can teachers exercise a full and proper professionalism when they are expected merely to implement an officially prescribed curriculum? What scope is there for the exercise of professional initiative, for risk-taking and the adventurousness that effective teaching now demands if, through the operation of a centrally-controlled curriculum, teachers are under pressure not to risk offence, to play it safe, and not to rock the boat? For all of these reasons, a centrally-determined core curriculum is considered to be retrogressive and to reverse the developments that have been taking place to strengthen the professionalism of teachers.

The professionalisation of teaching that is implied by thesis 6 is felt to be threatened in other ways. There is a widespread fear that, when responsibility for the shape of the curriculum is removed from teachers and vested in a central political agency, the nature of the curriculum framework that emerges will be professionally highly questionable. It is likely to be narrowly utilitarian; to reflect the 'back-to-basics' mentality which reduces the educational enterprise to a preoccupation with a restricted range of skills; to over-emphasise preparation for the work-place and the cultivation of vocationally relevant skills and attitudes at the expense of broader educational aims; and to concentrate so insistently on the assessment of achievement that the curriculum is distorted and trivialised by being equated with what is easily measured. In support of such judgements reference is made, for example, to government ministers' frequent reference to standards, to the emphasis devoted in official documents such as *The School Curriculum* to 'preparation for work', and the undervaluing of other activities, and to the ways in which local authorities are being expected, by Circular 6.81 and 8.83, to ensure that schools 'set out in writing the aims which they pursue through the organisation of the curriculum and in teaching programmes'. The requirement that schools should provide a written curriculum specification is seen as the local counterpart to the national initiatives that are taking place with regard to the devising of criteria and detailed objectives in the different curriculum areas. All of these moves are interpreted by the proponents of thesis 6 as deeply disturbing developments which undermine the professional expertise of teachers and ultimately impoverish the kind of education that schools provide. Ted Wragg of Exeter University has given expression to widely held fears by postulating 'Ten Steps Down the Slippery Slope to State Approved Knowledge'. The ten steps include the following:

Step 1 Centrally prescribed and approved aims
Step 2 Centrally prescribed time allocations
Step 5 Centrally prescribed objectives and teaching materials
Step 8 Centrally prescribed objectives, materials, strategies, test items (from the APU bank) and remedial programmes
Step 10 Dismissal of teachers who fail to deliver:[11]

That gloomy scenario is thought to be the inevitable outcome of the adoption of a very limited nature of accountability. It is referred to as 'utilitarian'[12] or 'contractual' accountability because it relates to the performance of duties specified in teachers' contract of employment. The key feature is that teachers are taken to be responsible for producing certain results, for ensuring that pupils come up to certain standards of achievement. As was noted in Chapter 1, this view of accountability reflects public concern about educational standards and it is not difficult to see how it accords with the introduction of a centrally determined core curriculum, the specification of detailed behavioural objectives, testing, and the 'league table' mentality which ranks individual schools in relation to their academic performance on public tests and examinations. However, the proponents of thesis 6 maintain that 'contractual' accountability is based on an extremely crude and misleading version of teachers' professionalism. They question whether the measurement of pupils' achievements and skills is a valid way of evaluating teachers' skills; and they reject the implication that the quality of education is to be judged simply by concentrating on what is precisely measurable. For these and other reasons a 'utilitarian' or, as it is sometimes called, a 'political' approach to accountability is considered to be unsatisfactory. It needs to be supplemented, if not replaced by, 'professional' accountability, in which teachers are answerable to their peers and are to be judged in the light of principles and standards of professional practice rather than pupils' results in examinations.

In short, thesis 6 maintains that the institution of a national curriculum framework would infringe the professional autonomy of teachers, would seriously damage the case for school-based curriculum development, would result in a narrow and professionally suspect curriculum, and would undermine the standards underpinning the professional accountability of teachers. How far is it possible to reconcile the case for a national curriculum framework with these claims?

At first glance there would appear to be an attractive compromise: both sets of claims might be met by accepting the case for a centrally determined core but allowing teachers, through a national forum or some other structure, to determine what that core should consist of. But why should teachers alone have this entitlement? A centrally determined core curriculum ought to reflect what a given society values; it ought to be demonstrably related to a view of the good society and to constitute the principal means by which young people will be initiated into that society. Teachers certainly will entertain beliefs about the good society and about how it may be realised, but they can hardly claim to be *the* moral authorities with a monopoly of wisdom on the characteristics of the good society. That is a matter on which all members of the community will have views and there is no reason why the views of teachers should prevail, although they will be as entitled as any other members of the community to contribute to the debate. John White, one of the most persistent advocates of the case for a national core curriculum, summarises this criticism of teacher autonomy in these terms:

. . . Decisions about curriculum frameworks are inescapably connected with *political* views about the nature of the good society. If this is so, then teachers have no professional expertise which justifies leaving these decisions in their hands. If there could be moral experts, then as long as we ensure that there were a sufficient number of these to make curriculum decisions in schools, I might be less alarmed than I am about teacher autonomy in this regard. But I do not believe in the existence of moral experts. Teachers, it seems to me, are not *qua* teachers in any better position than anyone else, postman and doctors or whoever, to make decisions directly affecting the shape and character of our society.[13]

In a different context the same writer concludes that questions about the general shape of the curriculum are political rather than professional: 'Curriculum policy is in no relevantly different position from, say, taxation policy or foreign affairs'.[14] In a democratic society major issues of public policy – and the structure of the curriculum is surely such an issue – are settled by parliamentary action. Parliamentary action, in Britain, includes consultation and the taking of advice, professional and otherwise. Indeed, a government might rely very heavily for advice on a formally constituted and widely representative group of educationists and others, such as the Consultative Committee on the Curriculum in Scotland, which exists to advise the Secretary of State on curricular matters. It is significant that the School Curriculum Development Committee recently established south of the border has not been given any such advisory function. Nevertheless, there is evidence that the government has attempted to look upon the enterprise of establishing a national curriculum framework as a consultative process. In its commitment to extensive consultation on this matter the government is recognising the limits of the professional autonomy of teachers rather than undermining that autonomy.

What scope, then, is there for the proper exercise of professional autonomy if ultimate responsibility for the shape of the curriculum rests with central government? The answer to that question depends on whether central government provides a precise curriculum specification including detailed prescriptions on syllabuses or a general curriculum framework. Clearly, if a precise specification is produced the scope for professional autonomy is very considerably reduced, almost to vanishing point. However, a general curriculum framework still leaves teachers with almost limitless scope for the full exercise of their professional skills and judgements. Within such a framework a very great deal of curriculum development work would require to be undertaken at the local and the school level on the content of individual syllabuses, its sequencing, teaching/ learning strategies, modes of assessment and much else besides. In these circumstances, in which teachers are fully engaged in the work of planning, implementing and evaluating learning experiences, there would be ample opportunity for experiment, for action research, for innovation, and for all that is currently understood by professional development. In all such work teachers would have to come to terms with a range of practical problems which call for the highest levels of professional skill and judgement and it is in the exercise of these skills and judgements that the professional autonomy of teachers is most characteristically exemplified. Indeed, it is conceivable that, given a clear curriculum framework within which teachers' professional activities were to be conducted, the quality of the educational experience offered to pupils might be improved. At any rate, given these professional circumstances, one of the strong implications carried by thesis 6 is shown to be unwarrantable: there need be no polarisation between a heavy-handed centralist control on the one hand and local teacher initiatives and grass-roots development on the other. School-based curriculum development and its corollary, the professional development of teachers, are both fully compatible with a centrally determined core curriculum framework.

Another of the fears expressed in thesis 6 concerns the possibility that a centrally determined curriculum framework might reflect a narrowly utilitarian view of education at variance with a professional consensus on the need for breadth in the curriculum. This very criticism has been levelled at some of the government's publications. Critics have detected in *The School Curriculum*, for example, an over-emphasis on preparation for the world of work at the expense of Social and Political Studies as well as Expressive Arts. It is clear that the present government is committed to ensuring that the curriculum is more closely related to the world of industry and commerce and to life in a technological society. Evidence from the Great Debate and from other quarters suggests that there is strong support for a development of this kind. In addition, TVEI demonstrates the strength of the government's commitment in this connection. However, there has been no suggestion in any of the government's publications or utterances that the curriculum should be exclusively preoccupied with such a limited range of objectives. The aim, in the words of Sir Keith Joseph, is to achieve 'a broad, balanced and relevant curriculum'.

There are two further ways in which a national core curriculum might be unacceptably narrow and therefore professionally objectionable. First, that curriculum might call for the inculcation of certain views and attitudes. It might be stipulated, for example, that Peace Studies should seek to win pupils' commitment to nuclear disarmament, or that Economics should do nothing more than extol the virtues of capitalism or free enterprise. What is professionally objectionable about such attempts to use schools for political purposes is that teachers would be asked to abandon their obligation to teach and, instead, to indoctrinate, 'to close pupils' minds on open questions'. A national core curriculum that made such demands on teachers would be totally incompatible with the professional standards to which teachers are committed. Fortunately, there is no support for using schools as agents of indoctrination. Furthermore, as long as the distinction between a national framework and the detailed content of syllabuses is maintained, and as long as the latter are regarded as the professional province of teachers, the conflict under consideration need never arise. And it is significant that, in the government's most recent White Paper (*Better Schools*, 1985), schools are criticised for restricting pupils' curriculum and denying them opportunities for work in the scientific, practical and aesthetic areas in the curriculum out of 'the mistaken belief, once widely held, that a concentration on basic skills is by itself enough to improve achievement in literacy and numeracy'. Yet that unacceptable narrowing of the curriculum was at least partly brought about by criticisms from such politicians as Rhodes Boyson that the basics were being neglected.

Finally, thesis 6 reflects a concern that a centrally determined core curriculum might consist of a list of detailed curriculum objectives towards which teaching would require to be directed, with a consequent narrowing of the curriculum to what is easily and precisely measurable. The distinction between a national curriculum framework and detailed syllabus content is helpful here. The operationalisation of general educational aims, the specification of objectives, and the identification of the criteria for their assessment are all professional rather than political matters. They call for the expertise that is the stock-in-trade of the teacher. A national curriculum framework should therefore leave teachers with the task of ensuring that the quality of pupils' education is not damaged by the requirements of assessment. That is not to say, as thesis 6 might be taken to imply, that the specification of objectives and the deployment of criterion-referenced modes of assessment are educationally suspect and do not have a proper place in curriculum planning and practice. The demolition work done by Lawrence

Stenhouse[15] and others on the claim that all objectives should be expressed in behavioural terms does not exonerate teachers from the obligation to clarify their educational aims. The approach to curriculum planning which involves the specification of objectives and criteria of achievement is a powerful and generative way of organising pupils' learning. Arguably, these techniques form an essential part of the professional equipment of the modern teacher. Moreover, to suppose that teachers can avoid the obligation to clarify as precisely as possible the skills and understandings they seek to cultivate and the criteria by which they propose to assess their achievement is to weaken very considerably the case for teacher autonomy. Fortunately, a national curriculum framework will not interfere with teachers' capacity to exercise this responsibility.

Conclusion

In this chapter the validity of the case for a core curriculum was tested in the light of six theses, each embodying a related group of criticisms of, or reservations about, a core curriculum. The analysis has shown that in nearly every case the criticisms could be reconciled with the arguments for a core curriculum based on a broadly defined framework and that, in the few cases where such a reconciliation was impossible, the criticisms were shown to be invalid. Nevertheless, the analysis also showed that a national curriculum framework must be qualified in several ways if certain valuable features of education and teaching are to be safeguarded. The means by which these safeguards might operate are considered in the next chapter.

References

1 G. H. Bantock (1971) 'Towards a Theory of Pupular Education', *Times Educational Supplement*, 12 and 19 March 1971.
2 J. S. Bruner (1966) *The Process of Education*. Cambridge, Mass.: Harvard University Press.
3 Quoted in Diane Ravitch (1983) *The Troubled Crusade*. New York: Basic Books.
4 Mary Warnock (1977) *Schools of Thought*. London: Faber and Faber.
5 B. Crittenden (1982) *Cultural Pluralism and the Common Curriculum*. Melbourne: Melbourne University Press.

6 Taylor Report, Department of Education and Science/Welsh Office (1977) *A New Partnership for our Schools*. London: HMSO.

7 W. Gatherer (1984) 'The Boss's Job', *Times Educational Supplement Scotland*, 25 May 1984.

8 G. Caston (1971) 'The Schools Council in Context', *Journal of Curriculum Studies*, Vol. III, No. 1, May 1971, pp. 50–64.

9 G. Caston (1971) 'The Schools Council in Context', *Journal of Curriculum Studies*, Vol. III, No. 1, May 1971, pp. 50–64.

10 Quoted in Adam Hopkins (1978) *The School Debate*. London: Penguin.

11 Ted Wragg (1980) 'State Approved Knowledge? Ten Steps Down the Slippery Slope' in *The Core Curriculum*. Exeter: University of Exeter, School of Education.

12 Hugh Sockett (1976) 'Teacher Accountability and School Autonomy' in *Proceedings of the Philosophy of Education Society of Great Britain*, Vol. 10 (1), July, pp. 58–78. Oxford: Basil Blackwell.

13 John White (1976) 'Teacher Accountability and School Autonomy' in *Proceedings of the Philosophy of Education Society of Great Britain*, Vol. 10 (1), July, pp. 58–78. Oxford: Basil Blackwell.

14 John White (1982) 'Three Perspectives on a National Curriculum' in *Forum*, Vol. 24 (3), Spring, pp. 71–3. Leicester: PSW (Educational) Publications.

15 Lawrence Stenhouse (1975) *Introduction to Curriculum Research and Development*. London: Heinemann.

4

Criteria for a Core Curriculum

Introduction

The discussion to date has shown that there are strong grounds for ensuring that all pupils, in their own interests and in the interests of the wider community, should be helped to acquire a range of skills and understandings while they are at school, and for that to be brought about specific curricular arrangements have to be made at national level. The discussion has also shown that the arguments against national curricular provision can be accommodated. However, most of these counter arguments have drawn attention to features of educational provision that may be endangered by the introduction of a national curriculum framework. These valuable features of an educational system can be protected by stipulating that any national curriculum framework has to meet certain requirements and to satisfy certain conditions. It is proposed that these requirements and conditions should take the form of a set of criteria against which any proposed curriculum framework may be evaluated.

That list of criteria should certainly relate to the content of a national curriculum framework but it should also relate to the context in which that framework is planned and managed. Every curriculum is embedded in a social and educational context, a milieu within which learning experiences are planned, implemented and evaluated. Arguably, the quality of a curriculum will depend on the structures that are created to support its planning and its maintenance. The same will apply to a national curriculum framework. Certain conditions have to be met to ensure that the curricular framework is set in an appropriate context. Accordingly, on the basis of the previous discussion, this chapter proposes a set of criteria for evaluating the composition of a national curriculum framework and for determining whether the context in which it is developed, managed and evaluated is appropriate. Inevitably, these criteria are fairly general. This chapter therefore generates from the criteria a detailed checklist of questions which may serve to sharpen the focus of discussions on a national curriculum framework for its defenders and its critics alike.

Criteria for a Core Curriculum

1   *A national curriculum framework should be determined by central government after the normal democratic processes of consultation.* Since ultimately a core curriculum reflects the values of a society, it is a matter of public policy and, like other such matters, should be determined by the democratically elected and representative body, parliament. Obviously, in forming a decision, parliament will seek to reflect the views of the public and will take advice from professional and other bodies in the normal way. The fact that the shape of the school curriculum is determined in this way does not necessarily conflict with the establishment of national curriculum development agencies for, while such bodies may have an important contribution to make to curriculum development, they do not have the political authority, although they might claim that they have the professional authority, to determine the shape of the curriculum.

2   *The centrally determined core curriculum should take the form of a statement on the overall structure of the curriculum rather than a detailed specification of syllabus content.* In Chapter 3 the case was made for the decentralisation of curriculum decision-making, for strengthening teachers' professional development through involvement in the planning and evaluation of pupils' learning, and for enabling schools themselves to play an active role in curriculum development. Clearly, the scope for local initiative and for school-based curriculum development is seriously and unacceptably restricted if the centrally determined core curriculum is specified in detail. What is required, therefore, is a set of principles covering the general shape of the curriculum. In this way, the claims of central

government, of local government, and of the schools themselves for involvement in curriculum development can all be reconciled: a national framework can be evolved which does not interfere with the responsibility of local education authorities to ensure that the curriculum is attuned to local needs and aspirations, and which does not deny teachers their responsibility to relate the curriculum to the particular circumstances of individual schools and to devise appropriate teaching/learning strategies for the classroom.

3   *The national curriculum framework should be derived from, and relate directly to, a set of general educational objectives which involve the skills, the understandings, the dispositions and values required for life in a democratic society.* As the previous discussion has shown, the analysis of the issues surrounding a core curriculum inevitably raises questions concerning the values underlying an educational system and the central purposes towards which it is directed. Too often, attempts to delineate a core curriculum amount to nothing more than the listing of compulsory subjects. Such attempts are unhelpful. They stem from a failure to recognise that subjects constitute resources that can be used to realise an almost limitless range of objectives: they may, for instance, constitute the medium for the cultivation of critical rationality, for the mere training of the memory, for inducing docility and passivity or resourcefulness, or for instilling a blind faith in authority, or the most profound scepticism and much else besides. A national curriculum framework, it is maintained, is a manifestation of a social and educational philosophy and a description of such a framework can make no sense unless it clarifies the central assumptions and values from which it springs.

The objectives of a national curriculum framework are inescapably social in character: they are bound to relate to the range of qualities and capacities that are required for effective participation in the life of the community. The term 'social competence' is a convenient shorthand for that range of qualities and capacities. Clearly, the range of such qualities is extremely diverse. It includes skills and understandings relating to oneself and other people, the dynamics of human development and social interaction, the development and nature of social and political institutions, family life, social services, the arts, leisure activities, the occupational structure and different forms of employment, the man-made and the physical environments, and the social and moral issues on which opinions differ in our society. The importance of such skills and understandings in pupils' education has been widely recognised and, indeed, their possession has been regarded as the hallmark of the educated person. Two recent commentaries on the work of schools have served to strengthen the connection between the curriculum and social life and to draw attention to aspects of social life that have been undervalued in the past. In the first of these Patricia White,[1] in an examination of the ways in which pupils might be more effectively prepared for life in a participatory democracy, advocates a curriculum that involves an analysis of human rights, obligations and opportunities; the distribution of power in society; and the political and inter-personal skills required for effective democratic decision-making. In the second commentary, a contemporary restatement of the aims of education, John White[2] maintains that, since education is directed towards social ends and to enabling people to participate fully in social life, high priority should be attached to the fostering of dispositions rather than the cultivation of knowledge. Of course, he does not imply that the possession of knowledge is unimportant: he concedes that all kinds of knowledge need to be acquired, not simply for its own sake, but as the prerequisite to engagement in social life and to the working out of a 'life-plan', the selection of the kind of life a person wishes to lead. The dispositions emphasised by White include cooperativeness, moral courage, independent-mindedness, self-directedness, reflectiveness, resourcefulness, tolerance, prudence and fairness. Whether or not the shaping of dispositions is to be exalted above the development of knowledge and understanding, both are clearly essential features of what has been termed 'social competence' and a core curriculum will therefore seek to ensure that both dispositions and cognitive learnings are cultivated.

Among the social objectives of a national core curriculum are those relating to vocational skill and understanding. As was noted in Chapter 2, the thrust for a national core curriculum was activated by the mismatch between the school curriculum and the world of industry and commerce: what pupils were expected to learn at school did not connect directly with the demands of a complex industrial society. Without in any way implying that education is reducible simply to vocational preparation, it is incontestable that the skills pupils are expected to acquire at school should take account of the world of work. The government's TVEI has demonstrated that highly imaginative projects can be devised which are designed to equip young people with the technical and social skills demanded by the world of work without abandoning the commitment to general educational objectives.

4 *A national curriculum framework should reflect a defensible categorisation of knowledge and forms of disciplined activity*. It was noted in Chapter 2 that human knowledge is divisible into a number of distinctive categories. While there are several categorisations currently available, they tend to be broadly similar: they each seek to reduce the diversity of subjects and disciplines into a limited number of divisions and they each seek to demonstrate the distinctive educational contribution that is to be provided by each family of disciplines. A national curriculum framework should certainly seek to ensure that all pupils have access to each of the distinctive areas of educational experience, whatever form of categorisation is used. Clearly, the use of some such categorisation system is a more powerful and useful way of identifying the areas of study to be covered than a mere list of subjects. Such a list could only be based on the distinctive educational contribution to be made by each of the subjects listed, but how can a claim to distinctiveness be demonstrated without recourse to an over-arching categorisation of knowledge? Unless such a categorisation is accepted, curriculum planning is reduced to unfruitful bargaining about the claims of Physics versus Chemistry, or of Art versus Drama and Music.

The earlier discussion showed that the aim of providing access to each of a number of distinctive types of disciplined activity is not merely to enable pupils to be knowledgeable *about* each area, for that would be to encourage the passive absorption of facts and principles. Rather the aim must be to engage pupils in the types of investigative and problem-solving activity that characterise the various fields of intellectual enquiry and reflection. In this way, pupils become not simply receivers of knowledge, but participators in a number of traditions of analytical activity which, in their different ways, involve hypothesising, the evaluation of evidence, experiment and criticism.

5   *A national curriculum framework should make provision for pupil choice and should maximise opportunities for self-directed learning.* The case for pupil choice rested on both psychological and moral grounds: on the one hand, pupil motivation and commitment can be enhanced if pupils are able to pursue those activities in which they have a marked interest; on the other, the making of such choices was seen as a modest way of cultivating the autonomy of the self-regulating adult. While the scope for pupil choice will obviously be considerable in the optional area of the curriculum, it is also possible to arrange for pupil choice within the core itself. A core that reflects distinctive division of study, each consisting of a number of cognate activities, facilitates choice of this kind. At the same time, as was argued in Chapter 3, provision for pupil choice is inadequate if it refers only, in the traditional way, to choice of areas of study within a given framework. The principle of pupil choice also implies a degree of self-directed learning in the sense that pupils, particularly in the middle and upper years of the secondary school, should be able to negotiate a pathway through a course and be able to choose which tasks and assignments to undertake as well as the rate at which they move through the programme.

6   *A national curriculum framework should include a strategy for taking account of variations in the rates at which pupils learn.* A core curriculum does not imply that all pupils should be marched at a uniform rate across the same rough terrain, for that is bound to penalise at least some pupils. Two possible strategies were identified to cope with this problem. On the one hand, minimum levels of competence might be pre-specified in each of the required areas of study; these would constitute the core learnings and when pupils, having received appropriate teaching and remediation, reached the required level of mastery in each area, their work in the core curriculum would be completed and whatever further work they undertook in school would be of their own choice. That further work, however, would constitute an extension beyond the core and would represent more difficult and demanding work for pupils. An alternative to that arrangement, adopted in parts of the Scottish development programme, would involve the establishment of parallel programmes, with pupils embarking on the syllabus that was most clearly attuned to their rate of learning and working. The

similarities between these two approaches are worth highlighting: both imply the careful delineation of objectives, the diagnosis of pupil difficulties and the provision of appropriate remedial help. In addition, both entail that certain minimum levels of competence are achieved in each of the required areas. However, while the first approach allows a pupil to abandon the core, once the required level has been reached, the second makes provision for pupils to develop their competence well beyond the minimum level.

7 *A national curriculum framework implies a national system of assessment and certification.* If a core curriculum reflects what are nationally considered to be central learnings, there ought to be a means of determining whether or not these learnings have been achieved and of attesting publicly to their achievement. The national assessment arrangements may take one of several forms. The defenders of local democracy and school autonomy are likely to see the most appropriate form of assessment as being school-based with appropriate moderation to ensure comparability of standards between schools and regions. However, external modes of assessment of the conventional kind cannot be ruled out, for, properly conducted, these contribute significantly to the objectivity of assessment and to the establishment of national standards. External assessment has, in the past, tended to entail a high degree of curricular prescription and it is possible that the advantages of both internal and external assessment can be enjoyed in a system which combines both modes, as is proposed in the Scottish reforms. Whatever form the assessment arrangements take, they ought to issue in a common form of certification which constitutes a formal and public attestation to what pupils have learned in the areas of the national curriculum framework.

8 *A national curriculum framework requires that appropriate procedures are adopted at national, LEA and school levels.* At national level provision has to be made for consultation on the shape of the curriculum framework; procedures are necessary for ensuring that the requirements of the national framework are unambiguously communicated to LEAs and that LEAs are carrying out their curriculum management responsibilities. In addition, the national arrangements for assessment and certification need to be properly documented and distributed by those with overall responsibility for

the education service. At LEA level there must exist a clearly defined policy, with appropriate supporting procedures, on the school curriculum. Such a policy and procedures should cover LEA requirements for the school curriculum, consultation with parents and other community groups, the communication of core curriculum requirements to schools, the evaluation of school curricula, the securing of properly documented curriculum policies in each school, including the demonstration of the compatibility of each school's programme with national requirements, and the provision of support for teachers, in the form of time and inservice training, to enable them to exercise their curriculum development responsibilities to the full. And at the level of the individual school there is an obvious need for the articulation of a whole-school policy on the curriculum and for the institutionalisation of appropriate procedures for its planning, management and evaluation. In these ways, central government, local government and the schools themselves contribute to the determination, implementation and maintenance of a coherent curriculum policy.

The Value of Listing Criteria

The identification of criteria relating to a core curriculum along the lines just attempted is a valuable exercise in at least two ways. First, it serves as a corrective to the tendency, detectable among critics and advocates of a national curriculum framework alike, to focus on a single dimension of the problem. The existence of a set of criteria governing the introduction of a core curriculum makes a nonsense of the claim that a core curriculum should be reducible to narrowly conceived back-to-basics priorities, or that it should consist of a mere list of traditional academic subjects, or that it will be a closely detailed curricular prescription which stifles teachers' initiatives. Secondly, the delineation of criteria should put an end to much of the current polarising of views with regard to a core curriculum. For example, we are not faced with a decision between central control and local initiative. There certainly must be central determination of the national curriculum framework but, as has been shown, local initiative in the shape of parental involvement or curriculum development work by teachers is essential to the proper conduct of schools. Another common polarisation of attitudes relates to the supposed conflict between the initiation of pupils into distinctive forms of knowledge on the one hand and the cultivation of what has been called social competence on the other. It is true that the forms of knowledge *can be* pursued in such a way that their relevance to the social realities of pupils' experience is extremely tenuous, if it exists at all; but the distinctive areas of experience or modes of activity do not need to be pursued in this way. Indeed, it has been maintained that pupils' social competence is to be fostered at the same time as pupils engage in different forms of knowledge. It is not a question of attending to pupils' cognitive and intellectual development in one part of the curriculum and then attending to the development of dispositions, attitudes and values, and social competence in the remaining part. Pupils acquire the various skills, understandings, values and dispositions implied by social competence in the process of being initiated into the distinctive categories of knowledge.

A further supposed dichotomy is that between education on the one hand and vocational preparation on the other. It has too often been assumed in the past that the work of schools should relate to one or other of these desiderata: either schools must be concerned with a broad general preparation for life or they should seek to involve pupils in a strict preparation for the world of work. It is surely obvious that if the purpose of schooling is to equip young people for the life they will encounter after school then it simply cannot avoid engaging them in the study of life in an industrial society and helping them to acquire the skills that will enable them to function effectively in that society. These and other supposedly inveterate areas of conflict are reconcilable and the proposed list of criteria is a way of reinforcing the conclusion that, even where different philosophies of education are to be found, there is a rational alternative to the form of educational inertia that consists of simply bemoaning the extent of our differences and disagreements.

The Development and Maintenance of a National Curriculum Framework: A Checklist

An alternative way of highlighting the factors that relate to the introduction and management of a national curriculum is to devise a checklist of questions that have to be taken into account in any such venture. The following checklist, which has been derived from the list of criteria described above, represents a more detailed elaboration of the eight criteria. The checklist has two parts: the first concerns the characteristics of the framework itself, while the second is concerned with its context, the factors relating to the origination, development, maintenance and evaluation of that curriculum framework.

Part A   The National Curriculum Framework

1   Does the national curriculum framework relate to a central core of learnings only, leaving a significant area of the total programme for optional or elective studies?

2   Does the national curriculum consist of a general curriculum framework rather than a precisely detailed specification of content for each syllabus area?

3   Does the national curriculum framework identify guidelines for teachers and curriculum planners on the principles which should govern the detailed working out of syllabuses?

4   Is the national curriculum framework derived from an explicit statement of general educational objectives and clearly related to these objectives?

5   Is the national curriculum framework directed towards the cultivation of the social competences required for life in a democratic society?

6   Does the specification of social competence include both dispositional and cognitive dimensions?

7   Are the values implied by cultural pluralism explicit?

8   Does the national curriculum framework take account of the diversity of roles people are expected to perform in modern life?

9   Does the curriculum help young people to acquire the technical, social and other skills required for life in a complex industrial society?

10   Does the curriculum make explicit provision for the development of an understanding of the social, economic and political aspects of modern society?

11   Does the national curriculum framework reflect a defensible categorisation of different forms of knowledge and disciplined activity?

12 Does the national curriculum framework seek to foster the investigative and analytical strategies of the different categories of knowledge and reflection?

13 Does the national curriculum framework make provision for pupil choice of activity within the various required areas of study?

14 Does the national curriculum framework afford sufficient scope for self-directed learning, for self-pacing and curriculum negotiation?

15 Does the national curriculum framework take account of the fact that pupils learn at different rates and require different kinds of remediation?

16 Does the national curriculum framework require that minimum levels of competence should be identified for all pupils in each of the required areas of study?

Part B   The Context of the National Curriculum Framework

17 Is the national curriculum framework determined by central government agencies?

18 Is sufficient provision made for consultation with professional and other public and representative groups?

19 Are the requirements of the national curriculum framework communicated unambiguously to LEAs?

20 Does central government have provision for determining how the national curriculum framework is managed at LEA level?

21 Has central government ensured that appropriate procedures exist for the assessment and certification of pupils' achievements in the national curriculum framework?

22 If the procedures referred to in 21 are not appropriate for the monitoring of national standards, have separate procedures for monitoring of this kind been developed?

23 Do LEAs have a clearly developed and articulated curriculum policy that is communicated to all schools?

24 Do LEAs require schools to generate a curriculum policy document setting out the strategies for planning, managing and evaluating the national curriculum framework?

25 Does the LEA have a clearly defined policy concerning support for schools in their curriculum development work?

26 Is provision made for parents and others to influence the LEAs

and the schools' interpretation of the national curriculum requirements?

27 Are teachers actively engaged in planning, managing and evaluating the curriculum in their schools?

28 Can schools demonstrate that their curriculum is compatible with the requirements of the national curriculum framework and its principles?

29 Can individual departments in each school demonstrate that their teaching and learning strategies are compatible with the principles embedded in the national curriculum framework?

30 Do the management strategies operating in the schools stimulate staff involvement in the continuous revitalisation of the curriculum?

31 Do schools have procedures for determining whether or not departments and individual teachers are implementing school policy on the national curriculum framework?

Conclusion

These, it would appear, are the types of question that have to be faced in determining the structure of a national core curriculum framework and devising the most effective ways in which it is to be managed. Without such a set of criteria or a working checklist it is difficult to evaluate the core curriculum or the effectiveness with which it is planned and managed. In the absence of clear criteria for judgement on these matters there is a strong possibility that practice would simply become muddled.

References

1 Patricia White (1984) *Beyond Domination*. London: Routledge and Kegan Paul.
2 John White (1982) *The Aims of Education Restated*. London: Routledge and Kegan Paul.

5

The Core Curriculum:
Three Contemporary Approaches

The criteria identified in Chapter 4 for the evaluation of proposals for a national curriculum framework, and the checklist devised from these criteria, were generated from an analysis of the arguments for and against a national core curriculum. That analysis sought to show that the arguments and counter arguments relating to a national core curriculum were reconcilable and that the polarisation of attitudes that is commonly encountered in this area is neither necessary nor desirable. The listing of criteria was seen as a way of ensuring that all the relevant principles could be brought to bear on the analysis and evaluation of any proposal for a national core curriculum. It remains, however, to illustrate how these criteria might be applied in practice. Accordingly, this chapter seeks to apply the criteria in an examination of three major sets of proposals for a national core curriculum – from Australia, from Scotland, and from England and Wales. Developments in these three countries are chosen because, in contrast to practice in France, Scandinavia, and eastern bloc countries where the content of the school curriculum is specified in detail by central authorities, they represent attempts to reconcile a national curriculum framework with diversity of educational provision, school-based curriculum development, and with demands for teacher autonomy.

Core Curriculum for Australian Schools

In 1980 the Curriculum Development Centre in Canberra, Australia, published proposals for a core curriculum for Australian schools.[1] The term 'core curriculum' was taken to refer to 'a set of basic and essential learnings and experiences', which formed 'a central and crucial part of general education for all Australians'. 'Basic' learnings were defined as those which laid the foundation for subsequent learning and personal development; 'essential' learnings were those 'which are required by all for effective cultural, economic, political, group, family and interpersonal life in society'. The CDC proposals were welcomed in Australia and elsewhere as an ambitious and imaginative attempt to establish, from first principles, a core curriculum for all pupils that went well beyond the basics to identify a comprehensive range of skills and understandings thought to be necessary for personal development and for life in a changing society. How do the CDC proposals measure up to the proposed criteria?

Criterion 1:   The CDC proposals were devised by a government-sponsored central agency – the CDC – and that agency, we are informed, developed 'close working relationships with state and federal departments and agencies, Catholic and other non-government school authorities, teachers and teacher educators, researchers, community groups and individual schools'. However, as they stand, the CDC proposals have no statutory force: they are purely recommendatory and are offered by their originators as a contribution to the public discussion of the issue. A national core curriculum must have stronger political validity than that: it requires nothing less than the authority of central government.

Criterion 2:   The CDC proposals were by no means intended to constitute a detailed specification for all that should be included in the core. The report openly conceded that 'It is not for the Centre to determine detailed curriculum content and teaching methods, or to prescribe syllabuses and texts. These are the responsibility of many different authorities and groups throughout the country, not least the teachers, parents and students in the schools.' At the same time, what was proposed amounted to more than a bald listing of required subjects. The essential areas of knowledge and experience are certainly set out but, in addition, it is stipulated that the core curriculum should engage pupils in certain learning processes which are intended to cultivate such skills and dispositions as the following:

Learning and thinking techniques such as problem-solving, lateral thinking, organised study habits, systematic recording of information, memorisation and recall, reaching decisions and making judgements;

ways of organising knowledge such as the use of themes and topics and ways of gathering and interpreting evidence, for example, in Science and Social Studies;

dispositions and values such as truth-telling, honesty, regard for others, and so on;

skills or abilities such as those found in reading, speech, the conduct of scientific experiments, elementary statistics, the use of tools, and ways of organising and completing learning tasks in groups.

These, indeed, may be seen as principles or guidelines according to which teaching and learning in the various fields should be conducted. It is true that guidelines such as these move beyond the notion of a curriculum framework. However, they cannot be said to stand in the way of school-based curriculum development or to deny teachers their professional responsibilities.

Criterion 3: The CDC proposals are based on an acceptance of certain 'universal aims of education'. Among the most fundamental of these are the following:

the nurturing and development of the powers of reasoning, reflective and critical thinking, imagining, feeling and communicating among and between persons;

the maintenance, development and renewal (and not merely the preservation) of the culture; that is, our forms and systems of thought, meaning and expression – such as scientific knowledge, the arts, languages and technology;

the maintenance, development and renewal (and not merely the preservation) of the social, economic and political order – including its underlying values, fundamental structures and institutions;

the promotion of mental, physical, spiritual and emotional health in all people.

It is recognised that these universal aims have to be interpreted within and for particular societies. In the Australian context they are thought to generate two further sub-groups of aims. First, there are those which derive from the values underlying the Australian way of life. These are taken to include the following:

a sense of personal, group and national identity and unity in all its people;

free communication amongst and between individuals and groups;

responsible participation in community and civic affairs;

tolerance and concern for the rights and beliefs of others;

equality of access to and enjoyment of education, health, welfare and other community services.

Secondly, there is thought to be a need for 'mastery of basic learning tools and resources'. These are taken to include the following:

communicating in spoken and written language;
number skills, mathematical reasoning and special relationships;
scientific processes and their applications;
logical enquiry and analysis;
creative, imaginative and intuitive ways of thinking and experiencing;
manual and other physical skills;
management of bodily and mental health.

These, together, constitute the general educational objectives which the core curriculum is intended to achieve. Clearly, that statement of aims fully recognises the social character of educational objectives. Besides, the development of social competence, with all that that implies, is seen as a central preoccupation in a core curriculum.

Criterion 4:   The CDC core curriculum postulates nine core areas of knowledge and experience. These are as follows:

1   Arts and Crafts
2   Communication
3   Health Education

4 Environmental Studies
5 Work, leisure and lifestyle
6 Mathematical skills and reasoning and their applications
7 Scientific and technological ways of knowing and their social applications
8 Social, cultural and civic studies
9 Moral reasoning and action, value and belief systems.

This categorisation does not owe any direct allegiance to any of the standard attempts by philosophers of education to reduce the various fields of knowledge and understanding to a limited number of distinctive categories. If anything, the preferred categorisation is reminiscent of the cultural analysis approach described in Chapter 2. Certainly, reference is made in the CDC paper to the need 'to make selections from contemporary culture and organise them into programmes of school learnings'. The nine categories listed show a need to take account of distinctive categories of knowledge on the one hand and of major areas of social life and experience on the other. One advantage of this approach is that it demonstrates the close interrelationship between what has been called academic knowledge on the one hand and social behaviour or 'action' knowledge on the other. No attempt is made to apportion the available time to each of these major areas, or to develop in any detail the ways in which they clearly interrelate. All that is insisted upon is that the curriculum of every pupil should involve work in each of these nine areas.

Criterion 5: While the CDC proposals clearly give schools very considerable scope for them to devise their own programmes within the general guidelines, the scope for individual pupil choice is not made clear. The document strongly suggests that there will be ample opportunity for pupils to work things out for themselves, to pace themselves through the programme, and so on, but no indication is given about the extent to which they will be able to choose from the various learning experiences made available within the core.

Criterion 6: The CDC proposal certainly makes reference to the ways in which pupils differ in the rate at which they learn but as they stand the proposals provide no indication as to how pupil differences will be taken into account in the core curriculum.

Criterion 7:　Similarly, no indication is given about whether or not in each of the required areas minimum levels of competence will be specified which all pupils will be expected to attain. Indeed, the way in which a national core curriculum might be reinforced by a national scheme of assessment and certification is not explored.

Criterion 8:　Finally, the CDC proposals, for all the richness of the curriculum thinking that underpins them, make no mention of the procedures at national, local authority or school level that will be required to ensure that the core curriculum is properly planned, managed and evaluated.

In summary, the CDC proposals appear to meet many of the items on the core curriculum checklist but do not take sufficiently into account considerations relating to pupil choice, to pupil differences and rate of learning, and to the ways in which pupils' achievements will be assessed and certificated. When judged in the light of the context of the core curriculum checklist (items 17–31) the proposals appear to be under-developed. They certainly recognise the need for consultation, they would allow schools and their teachers to be fully engaged in the business of curriculum development, and they appear to foster diversity of educational provision. These considerations apart, the CDC proposals demonstrate an almost total failure to recognise the importance of the context in which a curriculum must be set and of the procedures that are required if such a curriculum is to be properly managed and evaluated at national, local authority and school levels.

The Government's Development Programme in Scotland

The main features of the development programme in Scotland were briefly outlined in Chapter 1: the setting up of two national committees, one on curriculum and one on assessment, in 1974; the simultaneous appearance of the two reports in 1977, recommending a national core curriculum for 15–16 year-olds and a national system of assessment and certification covering the whole 16+ age range; the intimation, after public discussion of the issues and the emergence of a national consensus, of the government's development programme involving feasibility studies and the piloting of new curricula and assessment strategies in secondary schools; and the decision in 1982 to proceed to a phased implementation of the changes beginning in 1984. If anything, the decision to proceed to implementation led to an intensification of activity. Joint working parties, consisting of representatives from the Consultative Committee on the Curriculum and the Scottish Examination Board, were established in each of four new subjects to be introduced in 1984 and were given the task of drawing up draft guidelines for teaching and learning and for assessment in the areas concerned. Following discussion of the draft guidelines, final and official guidelines for syllabuses and assessment were issued in time for the beginning of session 1984–85. That process is being repeated for each of the subject areas that will be taught and assessed in the new Standard Grade, in a programme of implementation that extends to 1986, with the issuing of certificates covering all subjects in 1988.

The government's development programme in Scotland represents an unprecedentedly massive and ambitious undertaking, aimed at nothing less than a revolution in the curriculum and assessment arrangements for 14–16 year-olds in Scotland. While teachers and others have been, and continue to be, heavily involved in the development work, the whole enterprise has been led and coordinated by the Scottish Education Department. Not surprisingly, in view of the magnitude and comprehensiveness of the reforms, the Scottish development programme has attracted a good deal of attention from other countries, including south of the border. The Scottish documentation which articulated the principles underpinning the core curriculum has been complimented by a Parliamentary Committee as a more thorough and professional analysis than comparable documentation emanating from the DES.[2] Furthermore, since the development programme got under way and documentation relating to it became available, it has excited very considerable interest amongst DES officials, politicians and others. Indeed, there is no doubt that developments in England and Wales are being strongly influenced by the Scottish model of development. How, then, does that model measure up to the proposed criteria?

Criterion 1:   While education in Scotland has a separate statutory basis from that in England and Wales, the same ambiguity surrounds the question of curriculum control as is found south of the border. Traditionally, responsibility has been exercised by LEAs and by headteachers, although since the early '60s the Secretary of State has sought to influence the curriculum by endorsing publications of the Consultative Committee on the Curriculum, the Secretary of State's advisory body on curricular matters. The introduction of a national curriculum framework has been effected without resource to legislation: the Secretary of State has merely exercised a traditional entitlement to influence. Thus, the government's formal intimation of the changes took the form of a circular from SED (No. 10/93) which included these words:

> . . . All schools are asked to adopt the curriculum framework provided by the eight modes of study provided by the Munn Committee. Within that framework schools and education authorities are in the best position to judge the particular form which the curriculum should take in the light of each school's individual circumstances and the needs of its pupils. Nevertheless, there are certain overriding priorities and the Secretary of State considers that it is essential that all pupils in the third and fourth years of secondary education should study English, Mathematics and Science.

The Secretary of State's decision attracted some criticism because it seemed, by stressing the importance of three subjects, to represent a departure from the Munn framework which the Secretary of State is explicitly recommending. On that reading, the ministerial pronouncement is simply incoherent. The criticism is possibly based on a misunderstanding. The Munn framework, which posits a number of distinctive 'modes of activity', left schools considerable freedom to devise curriculum arrangements that were compatible with that framework. The Secretary of State has clearly endorsed that principle but has imposed the additional stipulation that, whatever strategies are adopted by schools to ensure that all eight modes of activity are represented in every pupil's curriculum, Mathematics, Science and English should certainly feature.

What is significant, in the present context, is that a national curriculum framework has been adopted that carries the authority of central government as represented by the Secretary of State. The Secretary of State's authority on this matter has been accepted, not out of docility or in the belief that the Secretary of State for Scotland is infallible in curriculum matters: it has been accepted because it is very obviously based on a clear national consensus. That consensus was reflected in the recommendations of the Munn Committee itself, which were, in turn, based on the evidence submitted to the committee. It was also reflected in the public discussion that took place following the publication of the report. Without probing too deeply into the reasons for the emergence of that national consensus – and the cogency of the Munn report's argument and the compactness of Scotland as an educational entity, cannot be disregarded in this connection – the existence of that consensus is beyond question and it undoubtedly made the introduction of a national curriculum framework a relatively unproblematic matter. The Secretary of State's announcement reflected what, in the light of the consultation and public discussion, local authorities and schools wished to see.

Criterion 2:   The second criterion relates to the perennial problem of central versus local control of the curriculum. The curriculum framework introduced in Scotland certainly gives schools the opportunity to interpret the national requirements in the light of local circumstances and of their own aspirations. However, the guidance to schools goes well beyond the provision of an overall curriculum structure. For each curriculum area guidelines are being developed and distributed. The guideline documents are substantial, extending to about 70–80 pages; each covers the aims of teaching the subject, syllabus content, teaching and learning strategies, modes of assessment, and the criteria to be used in the assessment of pupils' work; each is a comprehensive statement on the organisation and structure of a two-year programme of study and of the principles which should underpin the handling of the subject in the classroom. To what extent do these guidelines threaten teacher autonomy or school-based curriculum development?

Two observations may be made in reply to that question. First, the guidelines have been developed by groups of teachers and related professionals. Moreover, the guidelines were generated from extensive piloting of new curriculum materials in a large number of secondary schools and have been the focus of widespread discussion and consultation. Far from being a set of prescriptions cooked up by bureaucrats, the guidelines may be said to represent a professional consensus on how a subject can best be exploited to have maximum educational value for 14–16 year-olds.

Secondly, while each guideline document constitutes a wide-ranging analysis of the subject it does not prescribe every element in the curriculum. For example, the English document is quite explicit: 'The intention is to give departments freedom to design their own courses and course work assessment within a national framework.'[3] It is emphasised that the guidelines 'do not amount to a national external syllabus for English'. Indeed, virtually the only prescription that is made is that pupils' work in English will involve activities in the four language modes of reading, writing, speaking and listening, and an indication is given of the aims that should be sought in each of these modes. For example, reading is taken to cultivate pupils' capacity 'to learn to read for a variety of purposes and in appropriate ways'. That is taken to involve the following six purposes:

> to gain an overall impression, gist, of a text;
> to obtain particular information from a text;
> to grasp ideas or feelings implied in a text;
> to evaluate the writer's attitudes, assumptions and argument;
> to appreciate the writer's craft;
> to enjoy and obtain enrichment from a text.

Certainly, helpful suggestions are made as to the ways in which teaching and learning in English may be conducted and of the ways in which English activities may be assessed, but the onus for curriculum development is left squarely with schools themselves and their teachers.

A slightly different approach is adopted in Contemporary Social Studies, which, at the time of writing, is still at the consultative stage. It is proposed that the two-year course should consist of nine units as follows:

1 Industrial Society
2 Scottish Society
3 The Environment
4 Change in Society
5 Contemporary Issues and Problems
6 Contrasting Societies

7 ⎫
8 ⎬ Units to be selected and devised by schools themselves
9 ⎭

Guidelines for the first of these three modules are provided, together with the central concepts and teaching approaches. For the next three modules schools are left to plan for themselves what the detailed curriculum content will be, in the light of the general aims set for Contemporary Social Studies and the criteria to be used in assessment. Finally, for the last three units schools are again expected to devise syllabuses that are compatible with the aims and criteria for the course. Clearly, these arrangements allow schools very considerable scope for curriculum development and for teachers themselves to undertake development work in connection with the curriculum and its assessment.

In these ways the Standard Grade developments in Scotland seek to effect a reconciliation between what have hitherto tended to be regarded as irreconcilable demands: the need for central control of the curriculum and the need for school-based curriculum development. In Scotland a national curriculum framework has been introduced and central guidelines for each subject are being devised. However, the guidelines are developed by teachers and are intended to reflect enterprising classroom practice. Besides, within these central guidelines schools and teachers themselves are expected to exercise their skills and responsibilities for determining what pupils learn. Subsequent events have demonstrated just how real that expectation was. At the time of writing, Scottish teachers are working to rule, in a campaign to secure an independent pay review. As part of that campaign they are refusing to undertake the curriculum development work demanded by the new Standard Grade proposals, with the result that the Secretary of State has had to modify the implementation programme. If the guidelines actually specified what teachers were expected to do, Scottish teachers would have been in breach of contract if they refused to cooperate. They have been able to invoke the work-to-rule sanction precisely because the new proposals call for a considerable increase in curriculum development work by teachers.

Criterion 3:   The Scottish development programme rests on the analysis of educational aims undertaken by the Munn Committee.

That analysis sought to take account of changes in education and in the wider society and to articulate aims for secondary education in its contemporary setting. Four interrelated sets of aims were postulated:

1   the development of skills, such as the capacity to communicate, to solve problems, to interact with others, to make things, to perform experiments, and so on;
2   the cultivation of knowledge and understanding: the development of pupils' capacity to make sense of, and to think critically about, themselves and human behaviour, social structures and institutions, and the physical and man-made environments;
3   the fostering of attitudes, including such dispositions as a concern for others; a commitment to fairness, tolerance and rationality; openness to social change; a rational attitude to authority;
4   the promotion of social competence: the development of the skills and understandings relating to the central roles of adult life, those relating to work, to leisure, to family life and inter-personal relationships, and to membership of the community.

These aims were almost universally endorsed in the debate that followed the publication of the Munn report and, just as they provided the basis for the Munn Committee's curriculum recommendations, so they have been regarded as giving point and significance to the revitalisation of education for 14–16 year-olds in Scotland. They were derived from an analysis of what is involved in growing up and living in a democratic society and they are concerned with providing young people with the tools for autonomous decision-making in a social context. Besides, from the outset it has been accepted that the social functions of education are not to be attended to once the traditionally valued academic activities have received their proper attention. On the contrary, it has been maintained that each of the various components of the curriculum is at one and the same time a medium for intellectual development and for the cultivation of social competence. And in the reappraisal of curriculum content and approaches to teaching now taking place that principle is being fully acknowledged.

Criterion 4: The eight 'modes of activity' that form the basis of the national curriculum framework in Scotland derive, obviously enough, from the attempts by philosophers of education to reduce the very diverse range of disciplines to a limited number of categories. Each of the modes was seen as being distinctive, in the sense that it embodied a characteristic mode of investigation and analysis and, for that reason, had a distinctive educational experience to offer. The guidelines that are being developed for the different subject areas are attempting to ensure that each subject fully exploits the techniques of the mode or modes of activity to which it relates. In addition, subjects are being developed in ways which take account of the four sets of aims previously described. In this way, the contribution which subjects have to offer to the development of pupils' social competence is reinforced.

Criterion 5: The Scottish curriculum framework seeks to take account of the principle of pupil choice by allowing pupils to choose within the core as well as in the optional area of the curriculum. The arrangements probably allow as much choice as is compatible with a national curriculum framework. But how far is choice encouraged in the teaching of the various subject areas? In recent years, Scottish primary and secondary schools have attracted criticism because of their pedagogical restrictiveness: at both stages there has been an over-emphasis on didactic approaches. The subject guidelines currently being produced show an awareness of the need for diversity of approach and for exploiting opportunities for independent learning by pupils. However, to date, the guidelines have not gone as far in the direction of curriculum negotiation and open learning as the protagonists of these strategies would wish.

Criterion 6: The development programme in Scotland is intended to cover the whole age-range of pupils and to encompass everyone in the national assessment arrangements at 16+. The conventional educational wisdom would suggest that there are bound to be striking variations in the rate at which pupils learn. How are such variations to be taken into proper account? As was noted in the discussion of differentiation in Chapter 3, the Scottish response to this difficulty has been to posit in each curriculum area three different achievement levels – Foundation, General and Credit – at 16+, and to identify performance criteria for each of these (grade-related criteria). At the end of the two-year programme pupils receive the award that corresponds with their level of achievement. In some cases, for example in Mathematics, three separate but overlapping syllabus levels have been devised and pupils embark on the syllabus level that is most congenial for them, without pre-determining what level of achievement pupils will reach. In other areas, for example in English, there is no syllabus differentiation: pupils obtain the award indicated by their achievements during the course. This feature of the Scottish development has been criticised as involving a reversion to a highly divisive form of secondary education. However, its defenders maintain that syllabus differentiation is essential if at least some pupils are not to be penalised and that, so long as final awards are not predetermined, and pupils have the ability to move between syllabus levels, then the arrangements constitute a valid means of coping with the differences of achievement that are to be found when a national curriculum framework is introduced for all pupils.

Criterion 7: Criterion 7 stipulates that a national curriculum framework should be reinforced by a national system of assessment and certification. In Scotland, the curriculum and assessment changes are being implemented together and at all stages of the development since 1974 care has been taken to ensure not only that the changes in curriculum and assessment are compatible but also that they positively reinforce each other. It is for this reason that the guideline documents for the individual subject areas contain a detailed description of the criteria to be used in assessing pupils and of the general assessment arrangements and procedures.

One of the most significant features of these arrangements is that external and internal modes of assessment will be adopted and pupils' final grades will represent a combination of performance on external examination and performance in course work. In this respect an attempt has been made to combine two sets of claims: those relating to the objectivity of external examining and the establishment of national standards on the one hand, and those relating to curricular flexibility and the exploitation of teachers' professional judgements on the other. As a result, a nationally recognised system of assessment and certification is being introduced which attests to the level of achievement of all pupils in each area of the curriculum.

Criterion 8:   The educational compactness of Scotland has ensured that the national curriculum framework and the guidelines for individual subjects have been fully and clearly communicated to local authorities and to schools. The fact that LEAs and the various professional groups have been fully consulted with regard to these changes has helped to ensure that national policy has been readily understood and accepted. Indeed, the commitment to consultation has even enhanced the respect that is normally attributed in Scotland to circulars from the Scottish Education Department and the Scottish Examination Board. It is significant, however, that, in the massive documentation that these developments have generated, very little attention was paid to the ways in which the changes will be managed and evaluated. Welcome arrangements have been made for increased inservice provision to enable teachers and others to undertake the necessary curriculum development and related activities, but there certainly was very little, if any, attention devoted at the national level to the ways in which LEAs should evolve policies and strategies relating to curriculum management and evaluation. Even less attention was devoted to the ways in which schools ensure that policies and procedures with regard to the planning, management and evaluation of the curriculum should be evolved. However, somewhat belatedly perhaps, the SED has appreciated the importance of staff development for those holding important management responsibilities in schools and has made specific provision for these. In addition, the Department produced a report in 1984 on the management structures and strategies relating to all aspects of the work of the secondary school, including curriculum management.[4] That document certainly acknowledges that without attention to such management issues the changes that have been so long in the planning will not be effectively implemented and institutionalised.

England and Wales

The difficulty about undertaking an analysis of developments in England and Wales is that final decisions have not yet been reached about the shape of the national core curriculum and many related matters. In some ways, this inconclusiveness is surprising, given that the Great Debate was initiated in 1976 and that a whole succession of DES and HMI documents on curriculum matters has been released. These have all been regarded as discussion documents or contributions to the continuing policy debate. Even those that appeared late in 1984 – and others that are promised beyond then – are clearly not to be regarded as definitive. Whether this inconclusiveness is to be attributed to ministerial dithering or to a commendable commitment to consultation on intractable issues of public policy, it means that any analysis of developments must be provisional: it will be necessary to focus on what appear to be significant features rather than on a fully elaborated and definitive curriculum strategy.

Criterion 1:   In the succession of documents emanating from the DES and the Welsh Office since 1976 it has been repeatedly maintained that responsibility for curriculum is shared between central government, LEAs and the schools themselves. Nevertheless, the various ministerial pronouncements, the instigation of the Great Debate, the circulars exhorting LEAs to exercise their curricular responsibilities, were all clear attempts to engender a national consensus on the content of the curriculum without recourse to legislation. That strategy, as the Scottish experience demonstrates, was a reasonable one, for it allowed professional, industrial, political and other groups to influence policy while, at the same time, ensuring that the curricular framework adopted has the authority of central government behind it. It might be questioned, on the other hand, why the process should be such a protracted one and whether, in the search for a negotiated compromise, the commitment to a national framework might weaken and disappear. The latest document (September 1984)[5] is in some ways even more hesitant and uncertain than publications appearing in 1980 and 1981, confirming the view that the DES is making very heavy weather of exercising leadership in the progressive clarification of the central features of the school curriculum.

Criterion 2:   One of the recurring features of the official documentation is the disclaimer that central government has no intention of prescribing the detailed content of the school curriculum. That, the various reports make clear, and as Sir Keith Joseph has repeatedly emphasised in the press, is for schools and teachers to determine. The concern of central government is limited to securing agreement on a national curriculum framework and in that framework provision is made for an optional area in the curriculum of 14–16 year-olds. However, more recently, the present Minister has shown an interest in the content of individual subject areas and has made public utterances about Peace Studies, about whether Science should involve the study of the social implications of science, and about other matters. Moreover, details of the curriculum in individual subject areas are promised and the first two of these, dealing with English[6] and Science,[7] have just appeared. While these documents provide a less thorough analysis than the corresponding Scottish documents, they do seek to offer guidelines on the objectives that might be pursued at different stages. For example, the English paper suggests that 16-year-olds should be capable of reading literature of high quality, not restricted to the twentieth century, of writing job applications, and of adopting a critical attitude to the media.

However, the most significant development has been the publication, after two years of discussion between the Examination Boards, teachers and the Secretary of State, of national criteria relating to teaching and assessment in individual areas of the curriculum.[8] These national criteria form two categories. First, there are 'general' criteria, with which all subjects must comply. These stipulate that programmes in individual subjects must be free of political, ethnic, sexist or other forms of bias; they must reflect the linguistic and cultural diversity of society; they must seek to cultivate an awareness of economic, social and political influences on contemporary life; and they must be differentiated to take account of differing rates of ability. Secondly, there are subject-specific criteria which provide the basic principles underlying teaching and learning in each area. For example, the national criteria in English stipulate that the course should seek to develop the ability of students to:

> communicate accurately, appropriately and effectively in speech and writing;
> understand and respond imaginatively to what they hear, read and experience in a variety of media;

enjoy and appreciate the reading of literature;
understand themselves and others.

In the assessment of these general aims students will be expected to demonstrate their ability to:

understand and convey information;
understand, order and present facts, ideas and opinions;
evaluate information in reading material and in other media, and select what is relevant to specific purposes;
articulate experience and express what is felt and what is imagined;
recognise implicit meaning and attitudes;
show a sense of audience and an awareness of style in both formal and informal situations;
exercise control of appropriate grammatical structures, conventions of paragraphing, sentence structure, punctuation and spelling in their writing; and
communicate effectively and appropriately in spoken English.

It is stipulated, moreover, that students' programmes of work should provide them with opportunities to develop the skills of oral communication, to provide for pupils to undertake various types of literary texts and other materials, and to engage in a variety of styles of writing.

The generation of national criteria for teaching and assessing in individual subject areas may be interpreted as a most decisive shift towards central control of the curriculum. Is that shift so decisive as to undermine local authority responsibility in curricular matters and to deny teachers' professional responsibility for curriculum development? Three observations may be made in reply to that question. First, as was argued in Chapter 4, there is little value in stipulating that English or Science, or whatever, should form part of a national curriculum framework unless there is broad agreement about the kinds of activities that will feature as English or Science, or whatever. Secondly, the criteria which will govern teaching, learning and assessment in each subject area have been produced by teachers: they are professional, not politically derived, criteria. Thirdly, while the criteria are bound to reduce teachers' choice they still leave very considerable scope for teachers to devise materials and learning strategies that are appropriate for their pupils. In short, the national criteria do not constitute an unacceptable erosion of the professional autonomy of teachers: they provide an agreed framework within which that autonomy may be exercised.

Criterion 3: The educational aims underpinning the search for a national core framework in England and Wales were first enunciated in *Education in Schools* (1977). That statement, with some omissions and minor changes of wording, was reproduced in *A Framework for the School Curriculum* (1980) and again in *The School Curriculum* (1981). The following are the aims listed:

1 to help pupils to develop lively, enquiring minds, the ability to question and argue rationally and to apply themselves to tasks, and physical skills;
2 to help pupils to acquire knowledge and skills relevant to adult life and employment in a fast changing world;
3 to help pupils to use language and numbers effectively;
4 to instil respect for religious and moral values, and tolerance of other races, religions and ways of life;
5 to help pupils to understand the world in which they live, and the interdependence of individuals, groups and nations;
6 to help pupils to appreciate human achievements and aspirations.

This attempt to clarify the schools' central purposes has been widely criticised and dismissed, by John White, as 'intellectually decidedly shoddy'.[9] Critics have bemoaned the failure to derive educational aims from an analysis of life in the modern world, of the nature of knowledge, and of the values and qualities of the educated person. The impression has been created that the compilers of the documentation have ducked the responsibility to explore the complexities of the issues and settled instead for glib assertion. One indication of that glibness is the way in which, in the first of the aims listed above, the phrase 'and physical skills' has been added to the 1977 formulation, suggesting that the task of establishing educational aims has been interpreted as a matter of tidying up a draft rather than the demanding enterprise of developing a rationale from first principles.

A further group of criticisms insists that the rhetoric of the aims listed is a thin disguise for a political determination to reinforce the 'basics' and to force schools to prepare pupils more obviously and directly for the world of work. Undoubtedly, these two themes have pervaded the official documentation on a national core curriculum ever since Prime Minister James Callaghan's Ruskin Speech in 1976. And, certainly, the present government's Technical and Vocational Education Initiative, the sponsoring of programmes for pupils of 14+ that are closely orientated to employment, reflects what is taken to be the most pressing curricular priority – the bringing of the educational system into close alignment with the needs of the economy and of an industrial society. Without questioning the need for that kind of realignment or the standing of traditional academic activities, critics ask whether these important educational aims should be pursued at the expense of others that are just as valuable, and doubt whether priorities of that kind are fully compatible with Sir Keith Joseph's commitment to a 'broad, balanced and relevant curriculum'.

Criterion 4:   If educational aims are not fully and cogently elaborated, if the rationale for curricular activities is inadequately formulated and argued, it is scarcely possible to come up with a definitive curriculum structure. Certainly, such a structure is proving elusive in the England and Wales context. Indeed, a glance at successive formulations of the curriculum for 14–16 year-olds conveys a sense of continuing uncertainty and indecision.

1977 Curriculum 11–16	1980 A View of the Curriculum	1980 A Framework for the School Curriculum
the aesthetic and creative	English	English
the ethical	Mathematics	Mathematics
the linguistic	Religious Education	Science
the mathematical	Physical Education	Modern Languages(?)
the physical	Science	Religious Education
the scientific	Modern Languages(?)	Physical Education
the social and political	History(?)	'Preparation for adult and working life'
the spiritual	Arts	
	Applied Crafts	

1981 The School Curriculum	1984 Organisation and Content of the 5–16 Curriculum
English	English
Mathematics	Mathematics
Science	Science
Modern Languages(?)	Physical Education
Microelectronics(?)	'A worthwhile offering
CDT(?)	in humanities'
'Preparation for	Aesthetic subjects
adult life'	Technical Education(?)
Religious Education	Modern Languages(?)
Physical Education	Craft, Design and Technology(?)
'Some study of	
humanities'	
'Some practical and	
some aesthetic	
activity'	

What is to be made of these various attempts to delineate a national curriculum framework? It has to be acknowledged at the outset that in no case, not even in the case of those subjects that are thought to hold a 'key position', is there anything like a sufficient justification produced. There is no sense of a properly developed line of argument which might give a degree of coherence to the overall framework. Instead, there is a pragmatic and hesitant listing of essentials apparently in line with a developing consensus. That consensus appears to have established that certain subjects hold a 'key position' – English, Mathematics, Science and Modern Languages. However, the position of Modern Languages is ambiguous. Throughout the documentation there is a persistent refusal to come to terms with the issue of whether or not Modern Languages should feature in the curriculum of 14–16 year-olds. One of the 1980 documents claims that 'there is a strong case for a modern language in the education of all pupils'. Another concludes that 'most pupils should have the opportunity to become acquainted with another modern European language'. In 1981, it is suggested that 'wherever possible pupils should be encouraged to keep up a foreign language until the end of the fifth year'. And, finally, in the 1984 document it is asserted that foreign language studies should feature in the 11–16 curriculum 'for most pupils', despite the claim made earlier in that report that 'differentiation between pupils should, as far as possible, take place within, rather than between, the subjects they study'.

The ambiguity over Modern Languages is attributable to a failure to determine, from first principles, the educational benefits to be derived from Modern Language study. The case cannot be established simply by invoking Britain's membership of the EEC or the fact that people nowadays are able to enjoy continental holidays. If an activity is to occupy a compulsory place in the curriculum of pupils it is essential to establish that it has a distinctive contribution to make to their education. In the Scottish debate on this matter it was concluded that Modern Language study did not have a distinctive contribution to offer and therefore could not command a place in the core. Regrettably, however, the final decision may have been influenced by the irrelevant consideration that some pupils may not have the capacity to cope with Modern Language study. The debate in England and Wales seems to be showing evidence of similar confusion.

Ambiguities are to be found in connection with other components of the proposed framework. Paragraph 11 of the 1984 document makes it clear that government policy requires the inclusion of Physical Education in the core for all pupils to age 16. Paragraph 28 of the same document discloses that it is for consideration whether it should be made optional in years 4 and 5. A place in the national framework is found for Humanities but that place is not defended with any conviction or enthusiasm. Indeed, the wording implies that that place is conditional on the putting together of a 'worthwhile offering'. A similar uncertainty surrounds practical and aesthetic activities: their place in the framework is granted but the nature of their contribution to the total framework is left unclear.

There is one further feature of the documentation that is worthy of comment. That refers to the tendency to list the subjects that might appear in a national framework and then to conclude the list by reference to 'preparation for adult and working life', or 'preparation for adult life' or 'social education', 'environmental education', 'health education' and so on. The impression is given that the subjects listed will provide pupils with an appropriate education and, over and above what is derived from the study of these subjects, the school has to make provision for preparing pupils for adult life and the world of work and so on. There is a failure here to grasp that it is through the various subjects and activities of the curriculum that pupils are to be prepared for work and helped to come to terms with the demands that will be imposed upon them in a complex industrial society. Indeed, if the components of the core curriculum cannot be shown to be devoted to the achievement of these social objectives, they are merely contributing to that 'clutter' in the curriculum which Sir Keith Joseph is committed to excising. Perhaps these and other questions will be resolved in the further documentation on the school curriculum that has been promised.

Criterion 5:   All of the documentation relating to a national core curriculum in England and Wales recognises the principle of pupil choice and it is clearly intended that, whatever form the national framework ultimately takes, there will be a significant optional area. It is not yet possible to assess the extent to which the national framework will seek to institutionalise independent learning, curriculum negotiation, open learning, and other ways in which pupils might assume greater responsibility for the pace and content of their own studies.

Criterion 6:   How will the national framework take account of pupil differences? Sir Keith Joseph has made it clear that differentiation in the curriculum is essential, but, to date, the practical implications of that policy commitment are not yet clear. It is certain that criteria will be established in the different areas of the curriculum similar to the grade-related criteria established in Scotland. The establishment of such criteria for different levels of performance is a way of recognising that not all pupils will achieve the same standard. It also represents an acknowledgement of the principle that school assessment should seek to establish what standard pupils have reached rather than to indicate how their performance compares with that of their papers. The present government has a commitment to raising standards in schools and it is maintained that by specifying the objectives in each curricular area in greater detail and by focusing teaching on these objectives, the overall level of performance by pupils will be raised. Indeed, the objective set by Sir Keith Joseph is to bring about 80%–90% of all pupils to the level of achievement now reached by pupils of average ability in a number of subjects. Whether that is to be achieved by the provision of different syllabuses for pupils aiming at different levels of performance, or simply by more individually oriented teaching and learning strategies remains to be determined.

Criterion 7:   The commitment to criterion-referenced assessment and to the specification of national objectives corresponding to different levels of achievement will entail a national system of assessment and certification. That need not require the institution of a single school examining body, as is the case in Scotland, but it will mean that the activities of existing Boards will need to be rationalised and coordinated in the operation of national criteria and the determination of national standards. Accordingly, Sir Keith Joseph has intimated the introduction of the General Certificate of Secondary Education to cover the whole age range and to be administered by five groups of examining boards, four in England and one in Wales, instead of the twenty independent boards currently in operation. A major responsibility for the coordination of the national assessment arrangements will rest with the new Secondary Examinations Council.

Criterion 8:   Despite the inconclusiveness of the discussion relating to the content of a national curricular framework in England and Wales, it has been acknowledged that such a curricular framework will call for LEAs and schools to establish adequate procedures for planning, managing and evaluating the curriculum, for it is through such procedures that the accountability of the various partners in the educational service is to be demonstrated. While the documents already mentioned point to the necessity for such curriculum management procedures, two DES circulars (6.81 and 8.83) press LEAs and schools to clarify their practice in this connection. The circulars call on LEAs to evolve a curriculum policy, and to ensure that that policy is communicated to schools. They require schools themselves to evolve a curriculum policy, after consultation with parents and members of the local community; to set out in writing 'the aims which they pursue through the organisation of the curriculum and in teaching programmes'; and to make public the evaluation strategies they use. The irony is that LEAs and schools are expected to produce evidence of having established such curriculum management procedures in relation to the advice offered by documentation that leaves the structure of a national core curriculum indeterminate.

Conclusion

There are countries which find it acceptable to have the detailed content of the curriculum prescribed by central government agencies. In Britain there are strong objections to that degree of government intervention in the work of the schools. The thesis developed in this book is that, in a democratic society, some degree of oversight of the work of the schools is required and that such an oversight can be exercised, not by rigidly specifying in detail what schools should do, but by the introduction of a national curriculum framework which identifies the central activities that will be found in every pupil's curriculum. Such a national framework, it has been shown, is fully compatible with demands for school-based curriculum development, for pupil choice, for differentiation, for teacher autonomy, and so on. However, these desirable features of an educational system can be threatened by the introduction of a national core curriculum. They are to be protected, it is maintained, by stipulating that any proposed national curriculum framework should meet certain conditions. A set of criteria, deriving from the previous analysis, was proposed, and its use was illustrated in relation to three recent formulations of a national curriculum framework. The criteria may be used to assess the quality of the educational experience which any national curriculum framework will promote and to determine whether such a national curriculum framework will provide an appropriate context within which the skills and responsibilities of teachers can properly be exercised and developed.

References

1 Malcolm Skilbeck (1982) 'Core Curriculum for Australian Schools' in T. Horton and P. Raggatt (eds.) *Challenge and Change in the Curriculum*. London: Hodder and Stoughton/Open University.
2 House of Commons, second report from the Education, Science and Arts Committee (session 1981–2) *The Secondary School Curriculum and Examinations*. London: HMSO.

3 Scottish Examination Board (1984) *Standard Grade Arrangements for English.*
4 Scottish Education Department, A Report by HM Inspectors of Schools (1984) *Learning and Teaching in Scottish Secondary Schools: School Management.* Edinburgh: HMSO.
5 Department of Education and Science (1984) *Organisation and Content of the 5–16 Curriculum.* London: HMSO.
6 Department of Education and Science (1984) *Matters for Discussion, No. 1, English in the 5–16 Curriculum.* London: HMSO.
7 Department of Education and Science (1985) *Science for All.* London: HMSO.
8 Department of Education and Science (1985) *General Certificate of Secondary Education: The National Criteria.* London: HMSO.
9 John White (1982) 'Three Perspectives on a National Curriculum' in *Forum,* Vol. 24(3), Spring, pp. 71–3.

6

The Core Curriculum:
A New Synthesis

This book began by addressing a fundamental and perennial question: Who should determine what young people learn at school? A brief examination of the historical context of education in Britain showed that over the years very different answers were given to that question. In the 1860s, for example, the system of payment by results involved the rigid specification by central government of what pupils were expected to learn and financial sanctions were exerted to induce conformity to central government expectations. Throughout the present century there is evidence of a retreat from that strong degree of central control of the school curriculum until, on both sides of the border, a time was reached when responsibility for the curriculum was assumed to lie not with central government but at the local level. Indeed, in the immediate post-war years there was a fairly widespread consensus that headteachers and their staff exercised control of the curriculum subject only to such constraints as were exercised by external examining bodies and the entrance requirements of institutions of higher education.

The traditionally accepted pattern of responsibility for the curriculum began to be questioned throughout the 70s and into the 80s, and there is clear evidence of the growth of central government influence on the curriculum in these years. In this significant shift of government policy, repeated ministerial pronouncements asserted the entitlement of central government to influence the shape of the school curriculum and at the same time government action seemed directed to the elimination of institutions designed to foster curricular diversity and the introduction of machinery intended to strengthen central control.

There were several factors which led to the increased assertiveness of central government on curricular matters. There was widespread concern about the standards of achievement in the schools; representatives of the world of industry and commerce questioned the extent to which the curriculum equipped young people with the skills required to maintain the country's economic productivity; parents, politicians and pupils themselves questioned the relevance of the curriculum as a preparation for life in a complex changing society; and, on all sides, pressures grew for schools to be more directly accountable to the communities they served. Those pressures all combined to create a climate in which public confidence in schools was so undermined that initiatives on the part of central government to regulate the school curriculum were considered to be necessary.

The professional response to the increased ministerial interest in curricular matters was predictable. The system of payment by results had evinced strong opposition from teachers and engendered a deep-seated suspicion of, and hostility to, any move that even remotely resembled a return to the iniquities of that system. It was inevitable, therefore, that the growth of government interest in the curriculum should awaken traditional suspicions and antipathies and that opposition to the ministerial initiatives should once again be expressed. The arguments against central control of the curriculum were reasserted. Central control, it was contended, failed to take account of the principle of pupil choice in curriculum matters; it disregarded the fundamental educational principle that a programme of study should be carefully tailored to the pupils' capacities and to their rate of learning; it assumed, notwithstanding the evidence on the relativity of knowledge, that a national consensus existed on what pupils should learn at school; it failed to recognise that our pluralist society, in which a variety of different lifestyles and forms of community life flourish, presupposes a rich diversity of curricula rather than the rigid dispensation of a common diet to all; it conflicted with the right, in a democratic society, of individuals, groups and local communities to determine for themselves what pattern of learning experiences were appropriate; and, finally, it attacked what was considered to be the right of teachers as professionals to determine what was taught and learned in schools. In short, the ministerial initiatives were regarded as interventionist and as threatening that diversity of curricular provision which reflects the variety of lifestyles and communities in a multicultural society.

These developments might all be interpreted as a prelude to a classic confrontation in which the power of the state is challenged by those who champion the cause of pupil choice and differentiation, cultural diversity, local democracy and the professional autonomy of teachers. However, that analysis, which is evocative of battles over payment by results and its aftermath, seriously over-simplifies and distorts the contemporary situation. It is an obvious exaggeration to claim that the growth of central influence in the curriculum represents an attempt by the state to institute in a ruthlessly prescriptive way the precise curricular requirements for every school. The evidence very clearly points to the determination by the government, in Scotland as well as in England and Wales, to see instituted an agreed national curriculum framework which identifies the major fields of activity which all pupils should experience in their school years. It is clear that the national curriculum frameworks, both north and south of the border, are the result of an extended public debate, and that they allow adequate opportunity for pupil choice and curriculum negotiation, as well as for differentiation according to the rates at which pupils learn. These frameworks also allow different communities and localities to ensure that the curriculum in their schools is responsive to local needs and the requirements of community life. Finally, the fact that what is proposed is a framework rather than a fully elaborated curricular prescription acknowledges teachers' professional responsibility to plan the day-to-day learning experiences of their pupils. In short, it has been shown that a national curriculum framework need not conflict with any of these desiderata.

The three major national curricular initiatives discussed in Chapter 5 all exemplify these principles: in each case a national framework was generated after public and professional discussion. In the Scottish experience – and this is being replicated south of the border – certain guidelines for the treatment of the major components of the curriculum were evolved, based on ongoing work in schools and these guidelines will provide the context within which teachers will be expected to prepare detailed programmes for their pupils and will therefore be expected to cater for pupil choice, for the differentiated needs of pupils and to ensure that the curriculum is attuned to patterns of life in local communities.

It is legitimate therefore to refer to a new synthesis, in which the debate has moved beyond the rigid polarisations which set national against local government, politicians against teachers, and uniformity against diversity. The new synthesis rests on an acknowledgment that the framework of the school curriculum is a matter of legitimate public interest and must be determined by central government; at the same time it is recognised that provision has to be made within that framework for pupil choice, for pupil differences, for the type of diversity that reflects local requirements, and for teachers to exercise their responsibility for curriculum development. In the new synthesis there must certainly be a tension between what is determined nationally and what reflects local conditions, between the authority of ministers and the autonomy of teachers, between a national curriculum framework and curricular diversity. It is conceivable that within the new synthesis curricular provision is closer to one end of the continuum rather than the other. For example, the Australian initiative leaves considerably greater freedom to schools, to pupils and to teachers than do the national programmes in Scotland or in England and Wales. At the same time, even TVEI, which is widely regarded as evidence of a most determined interventionist policy by central government, allows very extensive scope for local initiative and for teacher autonomy. And the variety of approved projects confirms that judgement.

The new synthesis clearly offers a way forward from the traditional debate on the core curriculum. In that synthesis the traditional conflicts are reconciled through the institution of a national curriculum framework which reflects a professional consensus on the major components that should feature in every pupil's curriculum and indicates the criteria according to which teaching, learning and assessment within the main areas of the curriculum should be conducted. Such a framework undoubtedly recognises the traditional responsibility of local education authorities to ensure that the curriculum is appropriate to local conditions; it guarantees the critically important role of teachers in developing the curriculum for their pupils; and it makes provision for pupil choice and different rates of learning. The synthesis resolves the traditional conflict because it recognises the authority of central government while, at the same time, recognising the entitlement of others to influence the curriculum in individual schools. The balance of interest can be held as long as central government is restricted and as long as local authorities and teachers operate within the national framework. Educational provision, on both sides of the border, has long been regarded as a partnership between national and local interests. It is in the area of the core curriculum that that partnership faces its most exacting challenge.

Index